Advanced Distributed Scrum

A concise guide to building and leading remote
and hybrid Scrum Teams

Kelley O'Connell

‹packt›

Advanced Distributed Scrum

Portfolio Director: Pavan Ramchandani

Program Manager: Divij Kotian

Relationship Lead: Tejashwini R

Content Engineer: Esha Banerjee

Technical Editor: Vidhisha Patidar

Copy Editor: Safis Editing

Proofreader: Esha Banerjee

Indexer: Manju Arasan

Production Designer: Prashant Ghare

Growth Lead: Nivedita Singh

First published: July 2025

Production reference: 2170725

Published by Packt Publishing Ltd.
Grosvenor House
11 St Paul's Square
Birmingham
B3 1RB, UK

ISBN 978-1-83546-854-8
www.packtpub.com

Foreword

Scrum has always thrived on the power of small, empowered teams delivering extraordinary results. In today's hyper-connected, fast-moving world, that principle is more relevant than ever. Yet as organizations increasingly operate with distributed teams and flexible work models, traditional collaboration methods are being stretched to their limits.

That's why *Advanced Distributed Scrum* arrives at exactly the right moment.

Rooted in deep research, enriched with practical case studies, and filled with clear, actionable guidance, this book meets the needs of Agile practitioners facing the complexities of remote delivery. As **SAFe®** **Practice Consultant Trainers (SPCTs)** and with Darren also honored as a SAFe® Fellow, we've spent years helping global teams embrace Lean-Agile principles in distributed contexts. It's our pleasure to introduce this essential guide to Scrum Masters, Product Owners, coaches, and leaders navigating the new normal.

The book is thoughtfully structured in four parts:

- *Foundations of Remote Scrum* revisits the core principles of Agile and Scrum, then reimagines them for a distributed world, helping you instill the mindset and practices needed across time zones and cultures.

- *Team Building and Cohesion* explores how to find, onboard, and nurture remote talent. Psychological safety, trust, and shared purpose aren't bound by geography – this section shows you how to cultivate them virtually.

- *Technology for Distributed Team Success* dives into the enabling tech stack – from collaboration platforms to DevOps tooling and cybersecurity – ensuring your teams stay aligned, productive, and protected.

- *Remote Scrum Planning and Execution* provides practical adaptations of core Scrum ceremonies – Sprint Planning, Daily Scrum, Reviews, Retrospectives – so your teams stay energized, synchronized, and outcomes-focused, no matter the distance.

You'll also find rich case studies from organizations such as GitLab, Zapier, IBM, and Accenture, as well as dozens of real-world tips – from trust-building exercises to facilitation techniques to conducting remote performance reviews.

Whether you're a seasoned Scrum practitioner, a Product Owner aligning stakeholders across time zones, or an executive championing a global Agile transformation, this book will become a vital tool in your journey. Read it, tailor its guidance to your unique context, and turn remote work from a constraint into a competitive advantage.

Because distributed doesn't have to mean disconnected. In fact, it might just bring out the very best in your team.

– Darren Wilmshurst, SPCT, SAFe® Fellow

– Lindy Quick, SPCT

This book is the result of countless late nights, early mornings, and weekends spent bringing these ideas to life over the course of more than a year. It would not have been possible without the steadfast support and encouragement of those closest to me.

To my husband, Marc Desciscio, whose unwavering belief in me never faltered, even during the most challenging moments of this journey – thank you for being my rock, my sounding board, and my constant source of strength.

To my son, Nick, whose curiosity, determination, and spirit inspire me every day – you remind me of why I do this work, and you are always my greatest motivation.

And to my parents, Jim and Nancy O'Connell – thank you for instilling in me the values of hard work, lifelong learning, and perseverance. Your love and guidance have shaped everything I do, and this book is no exception.

With all my love and gratitude, this book is for you.

– Kelley O'Connell

Contributors

About the author

Kelley O'Connell is an internationally recognized Agile thought leader, author, and educator with a passion for helping teams and organizations thrive in an ever-changing world. With a career spanning over 25 years, Kelley has built a reputation as a trusted advisor to organizations seeking to unlock agility at scale, strengthen leadership capabilities, and empower high-performing teams.

Kelley's expertise is reflected in her extensive body of work, including more than a dozen courses and titles published on global platforms such as LinkedIn Learning and Coursera, where her engaging, real-world teaching style has attracted a dedicated global audience. Her work has been translated into multiple languages, making her one of the most widely followed voices in Agile coaching and leadership education.

Throughout her career, Kelley has held leadership roles at every level, guiding teams, programs, and enterprise-wide transformations across industries including healthcare, insurance, and financial services. A pioneer in leading distributed and remote teams, she has been practicing and coaching remote Agile collaboration for over two decades, well before it became mainstream.

As an Agile coach and consultant, Kelley partners with organizations to align strategy with execution, foster leadership agility, and build resilient teams capable of delivering lasting business outcomes. Her approach combines practical frameworks with a deep understanding of organizational dynamics, enabling clients to navigate complexity and achieve their strategic objectives.

Based in Chicago, Illinois, Kelley balances her professional life with a passion for travel and global exploration, continuously drawing inspiration from cultures and teams around the world. She welcomes connections and conversations with fellow Agile practitioners and leaders via LinkedIn, where she actively shares insights, tools, and stories from the field.

About the reviewer

Tarun Gupta is a distinguished Agile leader with over 18 years of experience in the IT industry, specializing in Agile project management, Scrum methodologies, and quality assurance. Holding a Master's in Computer Applications from Pune University, Tarun has cultivated expertise in software testing, project delivery, and Agile transformations.

His extensive certifications – including PSM II, PSPO II, PMI-ACP, SAFe Agilist, PMP, and Google Cloud Digital Leader – highlight his commitment to continuous learning and excellence in Agile frameworks. Passionate about fostering collaborative teams, driving innovation, and streamlining processes, Tarun excels in removing impediments and accelerating time to market.

In addition to his leadership in Agile practices, he has contributed to the review of *The Professional Scrum Master (PSM I) Guide* and *The Scrum Master Guide* by Fred Heath, both published by Packt Publishing.

Nick Kramer is a technology educator specializing in Scrum, Scrum@Scale, and enterprise agility. With over 15 years of experience, he helps professionals and organizations leverage emerging technologies and modern work practices to drive meaningful change. As the founder of One80Labs and One80Training, Nick has partnered with clients across industries – guiding teams in applying AI to enhance agility, automation, analysis, and workflow efficiency.

Ravi Sandhu is a Scrum.org Professional Scrum Trainer (PST), Certified Professional Co-Active Coach (CPCC), and product management consultant with over two decades of experience in developing digital, cloud-based and platform products.

Ravi has trained more than 2000 professionals globally, specializing in Product and Scrum. He is also a Rezoomex Certified Facilitator, where AI is used in generating smart contracts for businesses.

Ravi has successfully built many products with his teams for the UK Government and private companies.

He currently lives in Birmingham, UK.

Table of Contents

Part 1: Foundations of Remote Scrum

1

Introduction to Agile and Scrum   3

2

Principles of Distributed Scrum   15

Part 2: Team Building and Cohesion

5

6

Part 4: Scrum Planning and Execution

13

14

15

16

Sprint Review and Retrospective   177

Appendix

Using AI to Supercharge Scrum Teams   189

Preface

In a world where remote work has evolved from a rare exception to a daily reality, Agile teams are navigating uncharted territory. When the Agile Manifesto was first written, it envisioned teams co-located, collaborating face-to-face, and benefiting from spontaneous conversations and immediate feedback. Fast forward to today's globalized, digitally connected landscape, and the context has shifted dramatically.

Yet the core promise of Agile – empowering teams to make fast, value-driven decisions and adapt to change – remains more relevant than ever. The challenge is that these foundational frameworks were not designed with distance, time zones, or cultural divides in mind. Teams now need to revisit and reimagine how they apply Agile, particularly Scrum, to thrive in a remote setting.

This book is that guide.

Whether you are a Scrum Master facilitating Sprints across multiple continents, a Product Owner aligning stakeholders virtually, or a developer collaborating with teammates you may never meet in person, this book offers both a handbook and a playbook for success. It blends the timeless principles of Agile with the new realities of distributed teamwork, offering you practical tools, techniques, and strategies.

This book is organized into four focused parts to help you build, lead, and empower distributed Scrum Teams:

Throughout this book, you'll find actionable advice, real-world examples, and proven techniques to help your remote Scrum Team not just survive – but thrive.

Let's begin the journey to unlocking the full potential of distributed Scrum Teams.

Who this book is for

Advanced Distributed Scrum is written for Agile practitioners, leaders, and teams navigating the complexities of remote work in today's global environment.

This book is for the following:

- **Scrum Masters and Agile coaches** who are seeking practical tools and techniques to help distributed teams collaborate, deliver, and continuously improve
- **Product Owners and business leaders** who want to align stakeholders, manage priorities, and enable value-driven decision-making across geographies

- **Developers, designers, and technical team members** working in remote-first or hybrid environments who need to stay connected, productive, and engaged
- **Agile transformation leaders and change agents** driving organizational agility in remote or globalized enterprises
- **Organizations of all sizes** – from start-ups to enterprises – looking to optimize their Agile practices for distributed or virtual teams

Whether you are adapting existing Scrum practices for your remote team, launching a new distributed Agile team, or supporting a broader Agile transformation, this book offers actionable insights to help you build strong, high-performing Scrum Teams – wherever they are.

What this book covers

Chapter 1, Introduction to Agile and Scrum, explores the foundational principles and the streamlined Scrum framework to uncover the collaborative and adaptive approaches that empower teams to thrive.

Chapter 2, Principles of Distributed Scrum, delves into the intricacies of distributed collaboration by unveiling the essential principles of distributed Scrum.

Chapter 3, Roles and Responsibilities in a Distributed Scrum Team, explores the pivotal roles and responsibilities shaping the fabric of a distributed Scrum Team and provides insights into the nuanced dynamics of remote collaboration.

Chapter 4, Setting Up for Remote Scrum Success, lays the groundwork for triumph in remote Scrum environments by examining essential setup strategies and considerations to pave the way for efficient and collaborative distributed teams.

Chapter 5, Recruiting and Forming a Distributed Scrum Team, dives into the intricacies of team formation, recruitment, and onboarding, ensuring a cohesive and capable distributed Scrum Team that excels in remote collaboration.

Chapter 6, Cultivating a Strong Remote Culture, explores the nuances of fostering a vibrant remote team culture, promoting engagement, cohesion, and a shared sense of purpose among distributed Scrum Team members.

Chapter 7, Effective Communication and Working Agreements, explains how, through the art of remote communication and establishing robust working agreements, you can ensure seamless collaboration and alignment within your distributed Scrum Team.

Chapter 8, Managing Performance and Motivation, navigates the challenges of remote performance management and motivation, discovering strategies to keep distributed Scrum Teams inspired, productive, and aligned with organizational goals.

Chapter 9, Collaboration Tools and Software, unlocks the potential of collaboration tools and software to enhance productivity, communication, and project management within your distributed Scrum team.

Chapter 10, Remote Pair Programming and Code Reviews, teaches you how to leverage effective strategies for remote pair programming and code reviews, fostering collaborative development practices that ensure code quality and knowledge sharing.

Chapter 11, Continuous Integration and Continuous Deployment (CI/CD), explores the principles of CI/CD in the context of remote Scrum, ensuring a streamlined and automated development pipeline for rapid and reliable software delivery.

Chapter 12, Security and Compliance in Remote Work, addresses the critical aspects of security and compliance in a remote work environment, safeguarding your distributed Scrum Team and projects against potential risks and challenges.

Chapter 13, Remote Sprint Planning, explores how to master the intricacies of planning remote Sprints, ensuring a structured and effective approach to setting goals and priorities for your distributed Scrum Team.

Chapter 14, Conducting a Distributed Daily Scrum, covers how to deliver Daily Scrum meetings in a remote setting, fostering communication, transparency, and alignment among distributed team members.

Chapter 15, Sprint Execution and Monitoring, teaches proven strategies for successful Sprint execution and monitoring in a remote Scrum environment, ensuring progress tracking and timely adjustments for optimal project outcomes.

Chapter 16, Sprint Review and Retrospective, explains how to leverage insights from Sprint Reviews and Retrospectives to fuel continuous improvement within your distributed Scrum Team.

There is an Appendix at the end of this book. It covers notes and pointers on how to exploit the speed of AI to improve team efficiency and accuracy in planning.

Conventions used

Bold: Indicates a new term or an important word. Here is an example: Some common techniques you can use include **icebreakers**. There are myriad options you can find online; one of my favorites is "Would you rather?".

> **Tips or important notes**
> Appear like this.

Get in touch

Feedback from our readers is always welcome.

General feedback: If you have questions about any aspect of this book, email us at `customercare@packtpub.com` and mention the book title in the subject of your message.

Errata: Although we have taken every care to ensure the accuracy of our content, mistakes do happen. If you have found a mistake in this book, we would be grateful if you would report this to us. Please visit `www.packtpub.com/support/errata` and fill in the form.

Piracy: If you come across any illegal copies of our works in any form on the internet, we would be grateful if you would provide us with the location address or website name. Please contact us at `copyright@packtpub.com` with a link to the material.

If you are interested in becoming an author: If there is a topic that you have expertise in and you are interested in either writing or contributing to a book, please visit `authors.packtpub.com`.

Share Your Thoughts

Once you've read *Advanced Distributed Scrum*, we'd love to hear your thoughts! Scan the QR code below to go straight to the Amazon review page for this book and share your feedback.

`https://packt.link/r/1835468543`

Your review is important to us and the tech community and will help us make sure we're delivering excellent quality content.

Download a free PDF copy of this book

Thanks for purchasing this book!

Do you like to read on the go but are unable to carry your print books everywhere?

Is your eBook purchase not compatible with the device of your choice?

Don't worry, now with every Packt book you get a DRM-free PDF version of that book at no cost.

Read anywhere, any place, on any device. Search, copy, and paste code from your favorite technical books directly into your application.

The perks don't stop there, you can get exclusive access to discounts, newsletters, and great free content in your inbox daily

Follow these simple steps to get the benefits:

1. Scan the QR code or visit the link below

https://packt.link/free-ebook/978-1-83546-854-8

2. Submit your proof of purchase
3. That's it! We'll send your free PDF and other benefits to your email directly

Part 1:
Foundations of Remote Scrum

In this part, we will examine how Agile frameworks, particularly Scrum, empower teams to make design and execution decisions for their products. Agile was founded when distributed teams were rare. Given the rapid globalization of teams, it is essential that teams have a handbook and a tool kit to guide them in applying Agile and Scrum frameworks to the way their teams are working today. We will begin with a refresher on Agile and Scrum. From there, we will explore how these principles and techniques can be adopted and adapted by distributed teams.

This part has the following chapters:

- *Chapter 1, Introduction to Agile and Scrum*
- *Chapter 2, Principles of Distributed Scrum*
- *Chapter 3, Roles and Responsibilities in a Distributed Scrum Team*
- *Chapter 4, Setting Up for Remote Scrum Success*

1

Introduction to Agile and Scrum

The foundation of a successful product and project execution is a strong team. That is a challenging hurdle, even when your teams share the same office space. Now, when you consider that many, if not most, teams are distributed, the hurdle becomes even larger. Now, add the complexity of global time zones, not regional ones, and your challenges span the international date line. To conclude, "If you're a leader who is struggling to get the best from your distributed teams, whether they're near or far, you're not alone." Not only is there hope, but there are also techniques and solutions you can use to maximize the value of your teams.

In this chapter, we will examine why Agile practices, specifically Scrum, can help you solve these challenges. To master the techniques that will help you with your distributed teams, we must begin by gaining a deep understanding of Agile and Scrum.

In this chapter, we're going to cover the following main topics:

- Exploring the fundamentals of Agile
- The Agile mindset
- Introducing Scrum

Exploring the fundamentals of Agile

It's important to remember that Agile arose as a response to the traditional ways of working on products and projects. Refreshing ourselves on the traditional methods that gave rise to Agile is important. Only from this perspective can we acknowledge how bold these changes were and how dramatically they've changed our ways of working since 2001.

Methodology versus framework

The traditional method is generally referred to as the **Waterfall methodology**. This method reminds us of a waterfall because each step follows the completion of the previous step. There is no overlap between the steps. This order is the only order of execution. As shown in the following diagram, the flow of work is unidirectional:

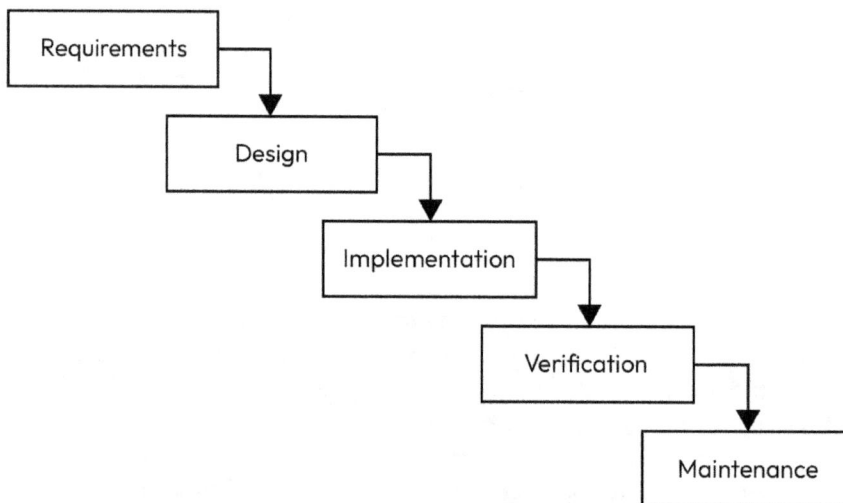

Figure 1.1 – Waterfall project methodology

Since this flow is one-way, there is no simple way to correct errors from a previous phase if you discover them after a phase has ended. This rigidity of this process is to be expected for a **methodology**. According to *Merriam-Webster*, a methodology is a body of methods and rules, a particular set of procedures. It's this rigidity that triggered the **Agile Manifesto**. Let's take a quick walk down memory lane. Before 2001, the vast majority of, if not all, projects and product work were being done while following the Waterfall methodology. There was no flexibility. The system used **defined process control**.

Defined process control means that, if you follow the process exactly, you will get the perfect, expected result every single time. Does that really happen? Of course not! The authors of the Agile Manifesto had already started rebelling against this notion and came together in 2001 to articulate what they were striving to achieve. To aid our exploration, here is the Agile Manifesto:

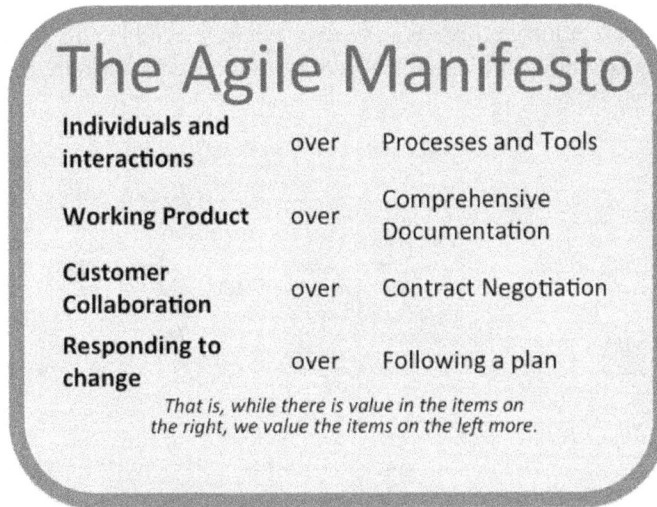

The Agile Manifesto

Individuals and interactions	over	Processes and Tools
Working Product	over	Comprehensive Documentation
Customer Collaboration	over	Contract Negotiation
Responding to change	over	Following a plan

That is, while there is value in the items on the right, we value the items on the left more.

Figure 1.2 – Agile Manifesto; Source: https://blog.itil.org/2014/08/what-it-service-management-can-learn-from-the-agile-manifesto-and-vice-versa/

We all know the Manifesto statement already, so I won't belabor its contents. However, one thing I would like to recognize is that this manifesto implicitly challenges the concept of defined process control.

You see, as developers who had been adhering to this control, they had discovered it consistently does not deliver what you expect, no matter how closely you follow the process. The items on the right of the preceding figure are defined process controls. So, what are the items on the left?

Those are the foundations of empirical process control. The shift is simply doing the work, looking at the outcome, and changing direction. That's what the empirical, or scientific, process is.

I cannot overstate how revolutionary this was and still is. While you and I know what follows, *The 12 Principles of Agile* fully defines what an empirical process looks like for software development. Let's look at them now:

12 AGILE PRINCIPLES BEHIND THE AGILE MANIFESTO

1 Our highest priority is to satisfy the customer through early and continuous delivery of valuable software.	2 Welcome changing requirements, even late in development. Agile processes harness change for the customer's competitive advantage.	3 Deliver working software frequently, from a couple of weeks to a couple of months, with a preference to the shorter timescale.
4 Business people and developers must work together daily throughout the project.	5 Build projects around motivated individuals. Give them the environment and support they need, and trust them to get the job done.	6 Agile processes promote sustainable development. The sponsors, developers, and users should be able to maintain a constant pace indefinitely.
7 Working software is the primary measure of progress.	8 The most efficient and effective method of conveying information to and within a development team is face-to-face conversation.	9 Continuous attention to technical excellence and good design enhances agility.
10 Simplicity – the art of maximizing the amount of work not done – is essential.	11 The best architectures, requirements, and designs emerge from self-organizing teams.	12 At regular intervals, the team reflects on how to become more effective, then tunes and adjusts its behavior accordingly.

Figure 1.3 – Agile Principles; Source: https://www.agilealliance.org/agile101/the-agile-manifesto/

Now, if you replace the word "software" in these principles with the word "product," you have a way of working that can be applied to any discipline or industry. You have – and the authors have – changed the world.

One final note about our illustrious Manifesto authors: at the time they met and produced the Manifesto, they had all been experimenting with different ways of working that would be the one and only "right" replacement for the Waterfall "methodology." So, in a sense, they were competing and trying to prove whose solution was the right one.

Ultimately, they decided they were all right. The compromise was not in deciding whose methodology was the right, best one – it was in understanding that no prescriptive methodology was right at all.

Instead, they called themselves "Agile" because they all wanted flexibility, adaptability, and the ability to pivot when needs changed. Then, instead of calling their ways of working "methodologies," which prevents those key things, they called their ways of working "frameworks." Instead of rules, there are guardrails to keep teams focused on the most effective ways of working.

We have a growing number of frameworks that live within the Agile family. Each framework has its benefits and drawbacks. You may find that some parts of **eXtreme Programming** (**XP**) are best for certain situations and **Kanban** is best for others. The most popular framework in use today by far is **Scrum**, so that's where we're going to focus our discussion.

"Lean"-ing Agile

The following is a brief note for you on the foundations of Agile. The Manifesto authors were very familiar with the manufacturing practices that emerged from Japan in the middle of the 20th century. These practices are known as **Lean manufacturing**, or simply **Lean**.

Lean has two primary focuses. First, Lean focuses on minimizing waste in a system. Second, it focuses on maximizing productivity. There's an inherent recognition that until waste is eliminated, productivity cannot be maximized.

The following diagram shows the focus on waste, specifically aligned to a manufacturing environment:

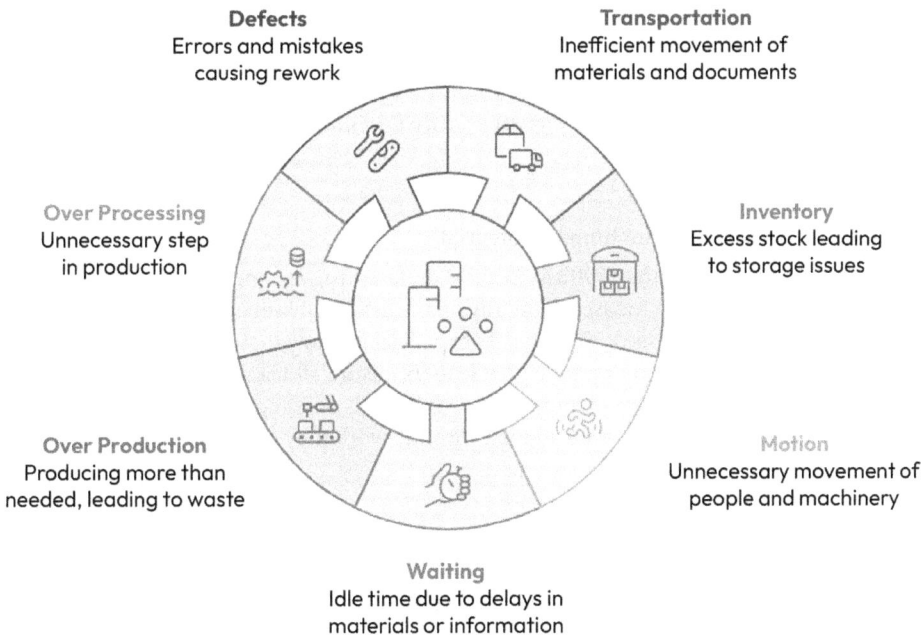

Defects
Errors and mistakes causing rework

Transportation
Inefficient movement of materials and documents

Over Processing
Unnecessary step in production

Inventory
Excess stock leading to storage issues

Over Production
Producing more than needed, leading to waste

Motion
Unnecessary movement of people and machinery

Waiting
Idle time due to delays in materials or information

Figure 1.4 – The Seven Wastes of Lean

The next thing that Lean demands is that value be defined from the customer's perspective. The customer is the person using whatever it is that we produce. It is the person who pays for what we are producing.

Software development is not the same as manufacturing, but the theory of waste and productivity resonates within technology and the software world, specifically. The authors of the Manifesto translated these Lean wastes into software development wastes. Here is what those wastes look like:

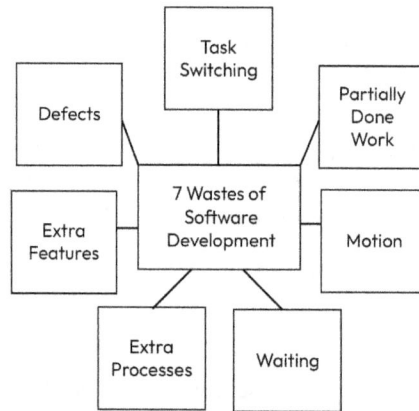

Figure 1.5 – Lean Software Development – 7 Wastes of Software Development

Now that we are aware of Lean, we can see how it influences our Manifesto and principles. Most important is the very first principle: *"Our highest priority is to satisfy the customer through early and continuous delivery of valuable software."*

> **A note on the 8th waste of Lean: human potential**
>
> This waste was introduced in the 1990's as Lean Manufacturing expanded beyond the Toyota Product System. This section is focused primarily on the historical influence of Lean and so this additional waste was not addressed. However, it's beneficial to know that this waste goes beyond the implied "idle resources" and demands that leaders ensure all team members' talents and abilities are harnessed in each Sprint and enhanced through ongoing training and education. Furthermore, individual skills must be aligned with the work they are doing.

The Agile mindset

The Agile mindset is a set of attitudes and values that supports the Agile family of frameworks. The mindset embodies all aspects of the Agile Manifesto and its principles. The focus is on flexibility, continuous improvement, and the importance of people. Here are the key components that define the Agile mindset. No matter which Agile framework you and your team choose, adopting this mindset is necessary:

- **Embrace change**: At the heart of the Agile mindset is the readiness to embrace change, even late in the development process. Agile practitioners see change as an opportunity to improve the product and increase customer satisfaction, rather than a disruption to avoid.

- **Value individuals and interactions**: Agile prioritizes people and the need for teams to work at a sustainable pace. Successful projects are the result of collaboration among well-organized teams who communicate effectively and do not require heroic efforts for value to be delivered. Team members should feel valued and empowered to make decisions, solve problems, and innovate.

- **Deliver working software frequently**: A key element of the Agile mindset is the focus on the continuous delivery of valuable software. Agile teams produce working products frequently, from a couple of weeks to a couple of months. The faster feedback that this approach offers ensures that the team is delivering what the customers want as close to the timeframe provided as possible.

- **Collaborate with customers**: Agile emphasizes close, ongoing collaboration with customers throughout the project. By involving customers in the development process, teams can better understand their needs and expectations, leading to products that truly solve their issues. It's also important to note that this collaboration is a negotiation between user needs and technical capabilities.

- **Respond to change**: Agility means being able to respond to change quickly and efficiently, rather than following a fixed plan. This adaptive approach allows teams to pivot, when necessary, based on feedback or changes in the market, ensuring that the product remains relevant and competitive.

- **Continuous improvement**: Through regular Retrospectives, teams reflect on what went well and what could be improved. They commit to applying these lessons in the very next Sprint. They're also open to sharing their lessons with other teams so that the whole ecosystem grows together.

- **Sustainable development**: Sustainability is the belief that teams should be able to maintain a constant pace indefinitely. This involves managing workload, reducing burnout, and ensuring that the team is working efficiently and effectively over the long term.

- **Simplicity**: Simplicity is the art of reducing the work to only the minimum required to meet the need. It focuses on what is essential to deliver value to the customer, avoiding over-engineering and unnecessary work.

- **Trust and empowerment**: The Agile mindset fosters a culture of trust, where team members are empowered to take initiative, make decisions, and take ownership of their work. This empowerment leads to more engaged and motivated teams.

The Agile mindset is not just about selecting and following an Agile framework. It's much larger and more difficult than that. It is about approaching work, life, and every circumstance with an attitude and approach that uses these key perspectives. When you apply this mindset and adopt it as your default operating system, you apply agility to everything you do.

Finally, we need to acknowledge and remember that Agile is a family of frameworks. All frameworks within the Agile family adhere to the Manifesto and principles, but they use different approaches to meet the needs of their specific environments and constraints. Here are the most common Agile frameworks you will encounter:

- Lean Manufacturing, or Lean for short, is one of the foundational Agile Frameworks. While there are striking similarities between Agile as a whole, and Lean as a specific framework, they are not the same. Lean primarily emphasizes delivering fast, eliminating waste, creating knowledge, building quality, and deferring commitment. Remember that when you defer commitment, you are maximizing the amount of knowledge at your disposal before you make a decision.

- Kanban is a framework based on Lean manufacturing. Its focus is making the work **visible**, establishing boundaries around how much work can be in process at a time, and maximizing the amount of work that can flow through the system.

- XP demands intense collaboration between the customers and the development team. It demands daily interaction to refine the requirements and minimal documentation since all parties are fully invested in the design and development of the solution. The challenge with implementing this framework is the level of discipline and endurance it demands from its teams.

- Scrum is the most popular and commonly implemented Agile framework. The focus in Scrum is on decomposing the project into multiple parts and delivering them in defined timeboxes known as Sprints. Each Sprint delivers an increment of the final project or product. Scrum is easy for teams to implement and notoriously hard for them to master.

Since Scrum is the most commonly used Agile framework, this is where we will focus our efforts. There are tools and techniques you can use with your Agile Scrum Teams to maximize their efficiency and delivery.

My Agile experience in a regulated industry

In 2010, the Affordable Care Act was passed into law in the United States. Features of these new insurance industry regulations were phased into effect beginning on January 1, 2014. At the time, I was working for a significant, national insurance carrier in the United States. Without going into too much detail, suffice it to say that every IT system for every health insurance company in the United States needed to make significant changes to meet regulatory requirements and avoid significant fines that were to be assessed per diem.

At the time, the IT organization was a fully traditional, or Waterfall, project management organization. When 50% of the compliance timeline had passed and only 10% of the work was completed, senior leadership recognized that something had to change if we were to meet the deadlines.

It was at this moment the CIO presented a radical proposal to shift all the compliance work from the Waterfall methodology to Agile frameworks – specifically, the organization moved to Scrum. All teams working on meeting the regulatory deadlines were trained, Scrum masters were hired, project plans were converted into roadmaps and release plans, and all teams started Sprinting simultaneously.

While I can't report that it went perfectly, the CIO of the organization, Susan Courtney, sums it up nicely:

> *I had it in my head that you couldn't apply [Agile] to very large projects, couldn't apply it in a regulated environment," she says. "It was amazing, the changes we saw throughout the rest of that year as we applied Agile principles and had the team work in a more collaborative way."*

> *[The organization] takes a slightly different approach to Agile than most organizations do, Courtney says. Instead of focusing on the procedure itself, she reinforces the thinking, culture, and mindset shift that accompanies Agile. "That's where we really saw the benefits," she says. "It was really in the essence of Agile and not so much the methodology.*

Kelly Sheridan, 2014, *An Agile Path To Success*, `https://www.insurancetech.com/management-strategies/an-agile-path-to-success/d/d-id/1317149.html`)

The CIO is accurate in attributing their Agile success to the focus on mindset and culture. As you attempt to level up Agile for your distributed teams, I highly recommend that you take this approach too.

Introducing Scrum

Scrum is an Agile framework that's designed to facilitate collaboration around complex solutions. As a member of the Agile family, it's founded on the Agile Manifesto and principles. From there, it branches into its own set of values and its specific practices. Scrum emphasizes adaptability and teamwork. It also calls for specific actions focused solely on the team and its need to continuously improve its processes to maximize quality and value.

Let's start by looking at **Scrum Values**.

The following are the five Scrum Values:

- **Courage**: Scrum Team members have the courage to do the right thing, take on tough challenges, and be honest about impediments. This value empowers growth and innovation.
- **Focus**: Everyone focuses on the work of the Sprint and the goals of the Scrum Team. By limiting distractions and multitasking, the team delivers higher value outcomes.
- **Commitment**: Scrum Team members personally commit to achieving the goals of the team and supporting each other. This fosters trust and dedication to continuous improvement.

- **Respect**: Team members respect each other's skills, experiences, and contributions. Respect creates an inclusive environment where everyone can thrive and collaborate effectively.

- **Openness**: The team and stakeholders agree to be transparent about work, challenges, and progress. This honesty builds a culture where problems can be addressed early.

The power and popularity of Scrum lie in these values. The Agile Manifesto and principles give us guidance on how we do the work from a process perspective. It sets the expectation that we need to prioritize customer value over everything else and the basics of how the team members work together.

However, the Scrum Values go further and tell us how we, be it as team members or leaders, need to work with each other. So, these Scrum Values focus on building a high-performing team culture where innovation, accountability, and collective ownership are the norm.

The basics of Scrum

Scrum simplifies complex projects and products by breaking them down into manageable pieces of work. Furthermore, instead of saying when the whole effort will be done, it talks about small spans of time, known as **Sprints**, during which a set amount of work will be completed, tested, accepted, and delivered. Scrum demands that we eat the proverbial elephant one bite at a time.

Scrum roles

Scrum defines three primary roles on the team:

- The **Product Owner** (**PO**) is responsible for maximizing the value of the product. The PO is responsible for "what" the development team delivers. They manage the product backlog and ensure that everyone understands the project's goals.

- The **Scrum Master** (**SM**) serves as a facilitator and coach, helping the Scrum Team adhere to Scrum practices, removing impediments, and ensuring that the team can work without interruptions. The SM ensures the team stays within the guardrails of the Scrum framework.

- The **Development Team** (**Team**) consists of professionals who do the work of delivering the product increment. They are cross-functional, with all the skills necessary to create a product increment. The team is responsible for "how" the development work is done.

These three roles are necessary for any Scrum Team to be successful. There is a push and pull between the roles. The PO wants to get as much from the team as possible, the team wants to meet the PO's needs, and, finally, the SM wants to help both roles by keeping them within the Scrum guardrails.

Without each role functioning well, the team will be out of balance and the product will suffer.

Scrum artifacts

Scrum has three primary artifacts for managing the work that's done on the product and capturing the requirements of the customers. These **Scrum artifacts** are as follows:

- **Product Backlog**: This is the list of everything the PO could think of that might be useful for the product. It is not necessarily a list of everything that *will* be done, but it is a list of everything that *could* be done. The act of prioritization by the PO will refine the Product Backlog log, shaping it into a product customers will want to use when it is delivered.

- **Sprint Backlog**: This is a subset of high-priority items that are selected from the Product Backlog. A new set of work is selected at the start of each Sprint for the team to fully focus on and deliver. Items that are completed and delivered at the end of the sprint are known as product increments.

- **The increment**: This is the set of completed and fully functioning Product Backlog items that have been completed during a Sprint and all previous Sprints. They must be in a usable condition.

The list of artifacts, or deliverables, for the Scrum Team is deliberately short. Delivering additional documents or features does not improve the product or ensure customer satisfaction. The goal is to refine and restrain the team to what is truly needed and asked for by the PO.

Scrum events

In the same way Scrum limits the number of distinct roles and artifacts, it also refines the number of events, or meetings, the team holds. Each event has a specific purpose and a specific timebox. This ensures that the development team's time is grounded in the product increment they are developing.

Next, let's examine each event in turn to understand how it serves the team:

- First, **Sprint Planning** occurs. This is a meeting at the start of the Sprint where the team decides what to work on during the Sprint. The work items are pulled from the prioritized Product Backlog and, once selected by the team, become the artifact known as the **Sprint Backlog**. The timebox for this event, as per the Scrum Guide, is a maximum of 4 hours per Sprint.

- Often, we forget that the Sprint itself is an event. By definition, it is the increment of time during which the team focuses solely on developing, testing, and delivering the work that was selected in Sprint Planning. A Sprint is generally 2 to 4 weeks in duration, with a preference for a shorter timeframe.

- Rather than weekly status or team meetings, a **daily Scrum** is held instead. This is a short, daily meeting (15 minutes or less) for the team to sync up. In this meeting, the team coordinates work being done, balances dependencies, and offers help where it's needed.

- The **Sprint Review** is the final public meeting of the Sprint. In this meeting, the team shares what has and has not been completed, plus any blockers that got in their way. The team and PO use this meeting to share progress with key stakeholders and to get feedback on what else might be added to the Product Backlog.

- Finally, the **Sprint Retrospective** (**retro**) is a private event for the team. This event occurs after the Sprint Review and before the next Sprint Planning session. It acts as a time for the Scrum Team to inspect itself and create a plan for making improvements to internal processes and standards. Each retro includes a commitment from the team on what they will improve in the next Sprint.

Summary

In this chapter, we explored the foundations of Scrum. We learned that Scrum grew from the ineffectiveness of the Waterfall methodology and was developed in a deliberate and targeted manner.

Next, our focus shifted from defined processes to empirical ones that are better suited to knowledge work, such as software development. Furthermore, we examined how Lean influenced the principles of Scrum.

When we explored the limited number of events, roles, and artifacts, we discovered the simplicity on which Scrum is based. Simplicity doesn't imply weakness, though – the framework is very powerful when applied well. Scrum's value lies in its flexibility, simplicity, and focus on delivering value quickly and continuously. It fosters collaboration and communication, both within the team and with stakeholders, ensuring that everyone is aligned with the project goals and progress. By breaking down complex projects into manageable tasks, Scrum enables teams to adapt to change quickly and efficiently, thus reducing risk and increasing the likelihood of project success.

Scrum is one of the most popular of the Agile family of frameworks Scrum, like all other aspects of Agile, is easy to understand but hard to master. To master Agile, you must change the way you think, both as a team member and as a leader. The Agile mindset, then, is the necessary foundation for maximizing the value of your distributed teams.

Much has been written about Scrum offering advice and suggestions on how best to implement Scrum with teams. Little, however, has been written regarding the changes you need to apply for remote teams. In the next chapter, we will discuss the practical challenges for these distributed teams and how you can alter your approach to best apply the Scrum framework.

2

Principles of Distributed Scrum

Traditional Scrum practices are challenged by the geographical distances inherent in distributed teams. Adapting Scrum for a distributed context requires a nuanced understanding of its principles and a commitment to preserving its core values. This understanding and application of Scrum at a distance must acknowledge that co-located Scrum is simply one approach to implement Scrum's inherent principles.

In this chapter, we are going to cover the following main topics:

- Adapting Scrum Values for distributed teams
- Communication in a distributed context
- Building trust across time zones
- Maintaining Agile Principles remotely

Through these discussions, we will emphasize the skills of flexibility, effective communication, and trust building. All of these are essential for the success of distributed Scrum Teams; mastering these skills will help you launch your teams for success in their distributed space.

Adapting Scrum Values for distributed teams

Scrum Values form the foundation of any Scrum Team, guiding behavior and decision-making processes. In a distributed setting, these values must be adapted to ensure cohesiveness and productivity. In this section, we are examining the foundational tenets of each Scrum Value. From there, adapting and applying these values to your distributed environment is essential to the success of your distributed team.

Commitment

In the simplest context, the Scrum Value of **commitment** means taking responsibility for the success of the product being built and the commitment made during Sprint Planning. This commitment applies to everyone on the team. At a minimum, it is focused on the Sprint promise and the individual's support of the product vision and goal.

When a team is co-located, it is an easy thing to see who is present, engaged, actively working, and focused on their commitment. This is harder to do when a team is distributed across time zones and locations.

In these cases, the commitment value needs to be refined to include a specific commitment to the team itself. Commitment to the product and the Sprint is impersonal; a person could work as an individual and meet this level of commitment.

However, in distributed environments, commitment to the team is a needed escalation of this Scrum Value. Commitment to the team includes being fully transparent on both work done and not done. It also means the team member is committed to ensuring their own personal Sprint and product success and doubly committed to the individual and collective success of all their team members.

Focus

Focus is about having a clear view and concentrating only on what truly matters to deliver the Sprint goal. It means working solely on essential elements and avoiding distractions that are not crucial to the Sprint goal. Further, it means delivering only what has been requested and not embellishing with features and functions that may be wanted in the future.

Again, this is an easy value to track when teams are co-located; it is not, however, easy from a time and distance perspective. Distributed teams need to enumerate how focus looks different from this perspective. On a distributed team, members need to be more aware during Scrum events of clues to watch for.

We are not policing each other's activities, but we are working to encourage focus and are asking our colleagues to help us in the same way. We are attentive to words that indicate an expansion of the task from its defined **Acceptance Criteria** (**AC**). Team partnership includes encouraging the right behaviors.

Openness

Openness involves being ready to share your knowledge and efforts, listening to others' ideas, and accepting feedback. It is about freely exchanging information among team members, making it easier for everyone to work and communicate.

In a distributed Scrum setup, where there are no collective tea- or coffee-break times, we must be more guided in how we pursue openness. These guided efforts can take many forms, from the simple to the complex.

For example, you may establish working agreements within the team on what forms of openness are typical for your team. You may indicate that there is at least one co-learning or collaborative design session each week or each Sprint. Additionally, you could require code demonstrations before a **Product Backlog Item (PBI)** is moved to **Done** on the team's Scrum board.

Respect

Respect involves appreciating diverse perspectives, listening to others' ideas, and providing support when needed. It means treating team members with courtesy and honesty and acknowledging the time they dedicate to the organization's success.

For teams distributed across the globe and spanning all cultures, the Scrum Value of respect assumes an even higher priority than for traditional, co-located teams who may share a similar culture. In the case of these broadly distributed teams, cultural differences can sometimes lead to misunderstandings.

Promoting respect, then, as with the other Scrum Values, includes some necessary modification. First, we must remember the purpose behind the value. When individuals feel respected and seen in their work environments, they deliver high-quality work and are more willing to collaborate with their peers. To achieve this, we need to foster an inclusive culture where every team member feels valued and heard. Further, each difference within the team needs to be acknowledged and explored for its unique enhancement to the team dynamic.

Courage

This Scrum Value can take many forms, and all of them should be encouraged. This value embodies the Scrum confidence to take risks. It encourages an environment where team members are open to learning from mistakes and developing new skills.

In distributed teams, an awareness that some cultures do not value openly acknowledging and sharing their mistakes is necessary. The team, to honor and maintain this Scrum Value, needs to establish working agreements defining what **courage** looks like on their team.

It may be disagreeing with the majority on story estimates or diverging on design recommendations. It may look like demonstrating a mistake that absorbed hours, simply so that others do not repeat the error. There are many ways courage displays itself on a Scrum Team; the important part is to ensure the team is communicating what it means to them and how they expect others to demonstrate it.

We are all familiar with the five Scrum Values. These values form the foundation of all Scrum Teams and guide their behaviors. In a distributed setting, these values must be adapted to ensure cohesiveness and productivity. In this section, we examined the foundational tenets of each Scrum Value. We offered solutions to adjust or adapt these Scrum Values, from its core tenets into a distributed framework. With these adjustments, you can ensure that Scrum Values remain the central core of your distributed Scrum Team.

Communication in a distributed context

When Agile first emerged, in various forms, in the 1990s, the vast majority of teams were co-located. That means they were physically located in the same office – perhaps not in the same area of the office, but it was easy to walk over and discuss design, issues, and errors. From this context, the Agile Manifesto tells us: *"The most efficient and effective method of conveying information to and within a development team is face-to-face conversation."*

Effective communication is the cornerstone of any successful distributed Scrum Team. A lack of face-to-face interaction can lead to miscommunication and delays if not effectively managed. There is no single communication technique that will work for every team, every time. There is, however, a set of techniques that, when applied to every team in a unique combination, will yield robust results.

Synchronous communication

Synchronous communication means that you are working together in real time. For some distributed teams, this is easier than for others. For example, for a team whose members range from Lisbon, Portugal, to Athens, Greece, synchronous communication is straightforward.

For other teams, it is far more difficult; for example, a team with members in Mexico City, Mexico, Kyiv, Ukraine, and Dublin, Ireland. Using tools such as Zoom, Microsoft Teams, or Slack for real-time communication helps bridge the gap created by physical distance. Regular daily Scrums and Sprint Reviews can ensure that everyone is on the same page.

These meetings should be as convenient as possible for as many team members as possible. When distribution is expansive, the team should explore the option of a rotating schedule where each time zone hosts daily Scrum and Sprint Reviews at their desired time. This rotation can occur every Sprint or every release; whatever the team determines will work best for them.

Asynchronous communication

Most people think synchronicity is the key to collaboration – hence all the meetings – but increasing asynchronous work can help your team become more cross-functional. It can also reduce meetings so that the ones you do have are more productive.

Asynchronous communication tools, such as email and project management software such as Jira or Trello, are crucial for distributed teams. They allow team members to communicate and collaborate without needing to be online simultaneously.

To successfully apply asynchronous communication, you need to know when it is the right avenue for communication. Use asynchronous communication in the following scenarios:

- Sharing status updates, meeting outcomes, and FYIs
- Sharing new processes or updates
- Shouting people out for a job well done
- Non-urgent feedback or input on non-sensitive issues
- Complex tasks or requests where people need time to gather their thoughts or information
- When schedules do not overlap

Use synchronous communication for these scenarios:

- Brainstorming or discussing complex topics that require several people's input.
- Sensitive topics such as client feedback and communicating major changes. Face-to-face meetings let you judge people's responses and adjust your tone and body language as necessary.
- When you can resolve something faster by talking.
- Emergencies and situations that require people's full attention; for example, getting your engineering team to fix a bug.
- 1:1s, quick catchups, and performance reviews.
- Team building activities such as games and icebreakers.

When your team decides which communication type is best for your situation, you can establish best practices and set expectations.

Clear communication protocols

Establishing clear communication protocols is essential. This includes guidelines on how and when to use different communication tools, response-time expectations, and documentation standards.

When people work on their own schedules, you need to set clear goals and expectations to keep everyone on the same page. This gives employees the freedom to choose when and how they do their work – as long as it is done on time and to standard.

Set expectations around deadlines, deliverables, and response times. Also, make sure your team is clear on individual, team, and company goals. This helps align their work with overarching objectives. You can also create and share guidelines on when to work async and in real time, how to communicate async, and which tools and channels to use.

It helps to follow teamwork agreements which must establish shared values such as accountability, transparency, and communicating the "why" behind requests. These help bind teams together and ensure everyone works together.

Visual aids and documentation

One way to maximize both synchronous and asynchronous communication is by using visual collaboration. Utilizing visual aids such as diagrams, flowcharts, and screen sharing during meetings can enhance understanding and reduce miscommunication. This type of co-creating documentation ensures collaboration across roles. Further, it facilitates both ongoing availability and accessibility to all team members.

As with all tools, you must choose the right tools for your work. For example, you would not use Microsoft Word to perform accounting calculations. Here are some tips for the successful selection of tools you might use on your team:

- **Visual work management**: Asana, Jira, or Trello
- **Document collaboration**: Confluence, Teams, or SharePoint
- **Visual collaboration and whiteboarding**: Mural or Miro
- **Design and prototyping**: Figma, Balsamiq, or Adobe XD
- **Collaborative software development**: GitHub or ProofHub

Finally, one of the most essential elements of using visual collaboration is to build a team culture around the tools. This includes training all team members on how to effectively use the tools and including this training when onboarding new team members.

Expectations should be set for when and how to use visual collaboration and documentation. It is common to see some level of documentation as a requirement for most Agile user stories. Including a visual element in those user stories or spike stories is an excellent way to reinforce your visual collaboration culture.

In this section, we have examined a set of techniques that, when applied selectively and creatively to every distributed Scrum Team, will generate robust team communication and collaboration. Effective communication is the cornerstone of any successful distributed Scrum Team. A lack of face-to-face interaction can lead to miscommunication and delays if not effectively managed, but judiciously applying these recommendations can enable your teams to succeed.

Building trust across time zones

One could argue that the unlisted but foundational Scrum Value is trust. The listed values of *commitment*, *focus*, *openness*, *respect*, and *courage* are all dependent upon a foundation of trust. Indeed, all teams require trust to perform well, and for distributed teams, establishing a foundation of trust is critical.

Barriers to trust

Establishing this foundation is necessary from the team's formation and requires ongoing assessment and nourishment for them to continue thriving. For remote teams, there are several reasons for difficulty in establishing trust; these are the most common:

- **Lack of face-to-face interactions**

  - This is a barrier to reading non-verbal cues such as eye contact, body language, and facial expressions, through which trust is built.

  - Informal, water-cooler conversations establish trust by enabling bonding on a personal level.

- **Limited visibility and accountability**

  - When you cannot see what others are working on, it is easy to assume they are not working at all. This perceived invisibility can lead to assumptions about others' productivity and commitment.

  - Accountability cannot be assumed; it needs to be pursued so that everyone is clear on how to measure colleagues' progress. Clear expectations and regular check-ins are necessary.

- **Cultural differences**

  - Diverse cultural backgrounds have varied communication styles, which can lead to misunderstandings.

  - Variations in work ethics, holidays, and expectations can create friction within the team.

These barriers may seem insurmountable, but they are not. When you apply proven techniques to establish trust from the moment of team formation, you can create a trusting team culture.

Strategies to build and maintain trust

Simply because it is difficult to establish and maintain trust remotely does not mean it is impossible. In practical terms, it means that monitoring, nourishing, and planning are required to create trust with your team. There are proven strategies through which to do this. Here are some for you to apply:

- **Regular communication**

  Beyond Scrum events, establish regular, one-to-one conversations with each of your team members, at least once per week. Hold these conversations over video to utilize both verbal and nonverbal communication. These are intended as more than just a way to give information transparently; they also ensure you are establishing a personal relationship with the team member.

- **Foster personal connections**

  Establish regular methods through which team members can meet socially. That could be a shared meal or a tea break on video. It could also include time to celebrate successes together with a game hour. The key is to ensure these occur regularly.

- **Provide cultural sensitivity training**

  It is important to acknowledge cultural differences on your team and embrace them. Formal, cross-cultural sensitivity training will be needed for most distributed teams. This training will ingrain understanding and respect for diverse cultures and promote inclusivity in your team.

- **Collaboration tools**

  Invest time in learning about your collaboration tools so that you can maximize the potential impact on your team. Everyone on the team should receive initial and refresher training on the tools, and there must be expectations established around which tools to use for what purpose.

One thing to remember when establishing best practices on your team is that collaboration tools are intended for collaboration, but they do not automatically enhance trust in the team. Do not rely on collaboration tools to replace the previous strategies listed. These tools are a supplement to those interpersonal activities.

It is not easy to establish trust in distributed, multi-cultural teams. However, taking the time and putting forth the effort is well worth it. You will create a trusting, efficient, and high-performing team.

Maintaining Agile Principles remotely

The Agile values of *commitment*, *focus*, *openness*, *respect*, and *courage* are the definitive guide on how Agile team members work with each other. The Agile Principles take that foundation further by defining how the team should do their work. While you are already familiar with the Agile Principles, it is always valuable to reexamine them and refresh yourself on their profound impact. You can read about them here: `https://agilemanifesto.org/principles.html`.

These principles can be boiled down to four essential categories, which you will need to ensure remain the focus for your team as they complete their work. Your focus on these will help you and your team maintain your agility.

Flexibility

Welcoming changing requirements is difficult for co-located teams where change requests occur in real time. For distributed teams, ensuring that changing requirements are shared immediately and transparently is essential. The goal is to mimic real-time delivery of information as much as possible. Furthermore, flexibility on a distributed team is reinforced simply by accommodating differences in time zones, work habits, and cultures.

Continuous collaboration

Maximizing your use of collaboration tools is key to ensuring this Agile principle remains at the forefront of your work. One example of a method for this is to maintain an always-open Teams or Slack channel where team members can reach each other easily.

Customer involvement

With remote teams, it can be more challenging to ensure every team member can regularly meet with customers. Spanning multiple time zones exacerbates the challenge; however, you can minimize the impact. Customers should always see the outcome of your Sprints at the Sprint Review, but that should not be the first or only time they see the work being done on their behalf. Hosting regular demonstrations of feedback sessions with your customers can keep your team members focused on and familiar with the customers they are serving.

Iterative development

The final category of Agile Principles is the focus on iterative development and how to keep your team moving forward using short development cycles. The goal is to build a solution and get immediate feedback from your customers. Pairing your short development cycles with the customer involvement we just examined can help reinforce the value of the Scrum Sprint cycle.

We have emphasized the skills of flexibility, effective communication, and trust building for your distributed Agile teams. All of these are essential for the success of distributed Scrum Teams. As you guide them toward mastering these skills, you will help them attain success in the distributed environment. Adapting Scrum to a distributed environment presents unique challenges, but with the right strategies and tools, it is possible to maintain the integrity of Scrum Values and principles.

Summary

In this chapter, we discussed how to adapt Scrum Values for distributed teams. We learned that these values do not need to be changed from their essential intent, merely adapted to ensure we are able to drive teams toward these behaviors more effectively. We also gained new skills to improve our effectiveness as communicators in a distributed context. Specifically, we learned when to use synchronous versus asynchronous communication and how to attain team consensus around acceptable uses of each.

Next, we examined the critical nature of communication in a distributed team. We defined ways in which adding visualizations to your ongoing communication with your team will deepen understanding and make it easier to remind team members of what has been discussed, designed, and decided. We talked about strategies for building interpersonal relationships and ensuring inclusivity on the team.

Finally, we reframed ways in which you can maintain all the Agile Principles remotely. We have proven that it is possible to adapt Scrum for distributed teams and attain the same level of high performance, camaraderie, and quality. From this foundation, we will move into tactics-related roles and responsibilities, where we will learn techniques to broaden and deepen the three Scrum roles of Product Owner, Scrum Master, and Development Team.

3

Roles and Responsibilities in a Distributed Scrum Team

The strength of Scrum comes from its simplicity. An essential element of that simplicity is the limited number of roles on the Scrum Team. Remember, the Scrum Team includes the Product Owner, Scrum Master, and Development Team. The effectiveness these three roles bring to the team depends on the clarity of the roles and the responsibilities that lie within them.

Those roles are difficult to master in a co-located work environment. In a distributed environment, the challenge becomes larger. Seamless collaboration, as we have already examined, is the foundation of a highly effective team. Mastering the nuances of the roles in a distributed environment will ensure successful outcomes. In this chapter, we will review techniques and approaches you can use to clarify roles and responsibilities on your distributed Scrum Team.

In this chapter, we will cover the following main topics:

- The role of the Scrum Master
- The Product Owner's responsibilities
- Working as a distributed Scrum Team member
- Distributed cross-functional collaboration

Understanding the role of the Scrum Master

The role of the Scrum Master is crucial to the success of every product team as it is the guardian of the Scrum framework and the team itself. Using the qualities and skills of servant leadership, or, as a leader who serves rather than directs, this role facilitates Scrum events and ensures adherence to the principles and values of Scrum.

In a distributed team, the role of Scrum Master becomes even more significant as they also take on the responsibility of creating a collaborative culture and nurturing the well-being of individuals to improve the whole. In this section, we are going to address the key skills that a Scrum Master must have to ensure their distributed Scrum Team is high-performing.

Servant leadership

It is easier to define servant leadership than traditional leadership. Traditional leadership roles focused solely on directing – or commanding – the work to be done, and controlling how the work was executed. The shorthand for this style of leadership is *command and control* leadership. This style of leadership intends to advance the leader's position.

In contrast, servant leadership inverts this power structure by investing the power in the people doing the work. This inversion of control shifts the focus to the team members achieving their goals.

This may seem to be an unusual, or ineffective, way to lead a team. It has, however, proven to be effective. Servant leadership, when in action, has two key behaviors that you can recognize:

- The first behavior is *removing impediments*. The Scrum Master is a keen observer of the habits and behaviors of the team. They are skilled at recognizing when something is a barrier to team progress and knowledgeable about when to step in and what actions to take to remove the impediment. These actions could range from addressing technical issues to ensuring proper communication is taking place.

- The second notable behavior is *supporting the team* to achieve its goals. While this may seem to be an innocuous activity that most teams could do without, it is not. Supporting the team includes more than cheering them on; it includes keeping the team members focused on their goals and objectives, remaining aware of the product vision, and providing necessary resources to help them attain those goals.

Finally, supporting the team includes providing guidance and feedback on how they are performing as individuals and as a team. *Robert K. Greenleaf*, founder of the servant leadership philosophy, said it best when he stated, "*Servant leadership always empathizes, always accepts the person, but sometimes refuses to accept some of the person's effort or performance as good enough.*"

Process facilitator

As the job title suggests, the Scrum Master is the owner of the Scrum practices within the team. It is significantly more complicated than merely hosting Scrum events. The Scrum Master ensures the Scrum framework's practices are followed. This includes the tactical activities of hosting and facilitating most Scrum events and ensuring they are being presented correctly.

Apart from monitoring Scrum events and artifacts, the more challenging aspect is ensuring the 12 Agile principles are followed and Scrum Values are being implemented by the individuals on the team. They begin by behaving in this way themselves. They lead by example. In doing so, they become the moral leader of the team.

Key skills related to process facilitation include using a variety of tools and techniques to ensure Scrum events and other meetings are productive. They use timeboxing techniques to facilitate and drive conversations to a conclusion or decision. Additionally, Scrum Masters are attuned to knowing when and how to bring in supporting visualizations.

One of the hardest skills to teach and most critical to have on a distributed team is the ability to negotiate within the team and mediate conflicts when they arise. The goal, from the Scrum Master's perspective, is to ensure all parties receive at least some of what they need from the issue's resolution. On distributed teams, communication and cultural differences can create significant challenges and conflicts are likely to arise. Having a Scrum Master who is skilled in conflict resolution can help the team succeed where failure may have otherwise occurred.

Finally, part of the process facilitation work is to ensure that work is coordinated within the team across the technical specialties of the individuals. Such activities that would take place here include facilitating discussions across the disciplines and acting as a liaison among designers, developers, testers, and the Product Owner.

A final aspect of the process facilitator's responsibility is the need to coordinate efforts across teams. No team, distributed or not, exists in a vacuum. Their work, when it affects the corporate ecosystem, will inevitably affect other teams. The Scrum Master is expected to attend Scrum of Scrums meetings with fellow Scrum Masters to coordinate work across the ecosystem. They are also expected to ensure the various Product Owners are aware of all products and touchpoints across the portfolio.

Outcomes of a skilled distributed team Scrum Master

When a Scrum Master is performing their role effectively, the results will be evident. To be, or assess the ability of, an excellent Scrum Master, look for these outcomes:

- **Clear communication and coordination**

  - Regularly scheduled Scrum meetings with published agendas and specific goals.

  - Effective facilitation where contributions are equal and balanced across attendees.

  - Events run smoothly and have active participation and clear action item follow-ups.

  - Efficient use of tools is an unrecognized way in which time is wasted in meetings and Scrum events. When the facilitator lacks effective skills in the tools being used, time is lost by everyone involved.

- **Proactive impediment removal**

  - A skilled Scrum Master spends a portion of each day considering the work of the team in the context of the corporate ecosystem. When they do this, they will identify risks that may become impediments. Following the nature of Scrum, though, the Scrum Master does not create detailed risk management plans. Rather, they consider potential disruptions and make note of them.

  - That forethought leads to the next demonstration of the Scrum Master's ability, and that is the skill of adaptability. The Scrum Master must be such an expert in Scrum that when impediments and changes arise, they are ready to act and steer the team through the challenge.

- **Fostering team culture**

  - The Scrum Master, as part of the embodiment of Scrum Values, creates an inclusive environment for everyone on the team. Each person should feel valued, seen, and heard. By ensuring all voices are heard in meetings and Scrum events, the Scrum Master ensures the team comes together as a healthy whole.

  - Teaching self-organization is not typically done; rather, the Scrum Master instills self-organization into the team by challenging them to solve problems themselves. The product solutions and the "how" of the product are owned by the Development Team; however, it may be new for them to design their own solutions. Encouraging and fostering self-organization includes technical design and having them take ownership of their work.

  - Continuous improvement is a crucial skill for the Scrum Master to demonstrate. Hosting regular Retrospectives will help the team achieve greater outcomes by encouraging the identification of actionable insights for targeted improvements. Additionally, the Scrum Master seeks feedback on their actions and abilities. Demonstrating a desire for ongoing personal growth sets an example for all team members.

The Scrum Master, as the process owner for the team, has a broad set of responsibilities. When these responsibilities are handed down deftly, a distributed team is empowered to succeed. Leveraging each of these skills and continuing to hone them, will ensure the distributed Scrum Team is cohesive and productive.

Examining the Product Owner's responsibilities

The Product Owner is responsible for ensuring the product delivers the value the stakeholders have requested. This pivotal role ensures that the team is delivering value to the business stakeholders and customers. The Product Owner must complete two key activities to ensure value is delivered: define the product vision and undertake stakeholder management.

Vision setting

Multiple steps are involved in vision setting. Most of the Product Owner's time is spent with customers and doing market research. That work, of product discovery and definition, is beyond the scope of this book. This book presumes that the Product Owner has already completed this investigative research and now has a product defined for the team to build.

Defining the vision includes all the essential elements of "what our product does, for whom, and why it is valuable to them." While this can be, and should be, summed up in an elevator pitch, more is needed to motivate the team.

The vision needs to be clear and compelling. It needs to inspire the team's efforts and gain emotional buy-in from them. This is the very first, necessary step in getting them committed to the product.

A compelling vision is also essential to keep and maintain stakeholder engagement. Every product journey, from idea to delivery, depends on the involvement of stakeholders and their commitment to keeping the Product Owner's vision of the future at the forefront of their minds.

One way to keep this vision and the product journey front and center for the team and stakeholders is the ongoing development, refinement, and management of the Product Backlog. It is a list of user stories, or requirements, of all the items that could add value to the product for the customer.

The Product Owner focuses on keeping the backlog organized and prioritized by the value it will deliver to the customer. These user stories are the result of regular meetings with the key stakeholders to ensure all valuable ideas are captured and prioritized based on their input. This ongoing interaction creates additional opportunities for the Product Owner to remind these key individuals of the larger product vision. When the Product Owner links the activities of vision setting and reinforcement with the solicitation of new requirements, the product will receive all the support it needs.

Stakeholder management

The Product Owner is the primary liaison between the team and the stakeholders. Stakeholders should not reach out to individual team members to get their favorite requirements added to the backlog or a Sprint. The Product Owner, then, is the gatekeeper to the features included in the product.

Ongoing requirement elicitation is one aspect of stakeholder management, and there are more. As product increments are delivered, the Product Owner ensures that the stakeholders see the increment and asks for their feedback. Input on what has been delivered and additional features that might enhance the increment are valuable inputs for the Product Owner.

Finally, while gaining feedback and adding and modifying story requirements in the Product Backlog, there is a need to keep the pulse of business value in the organization. Each stakeholder may have their preferences for which features are valuable, so Product Owners must collate all the feedback to assemble a backlog that will deliver the most value possible to the greatest number of stakeholders.

Outcomes of a skilled distributed Product Owner

When a Product Owner is performing their role effectively, the results will be evident. To be, or to assess the ability of, an excellent Product Owner, look for these outcomes:

- **Clear communication and coordination**: Regularly scheduled and structured updates for both the team and the stakeholders. Both groups need to understand the product's progress in comparison to the vision. Business needs change, so the vision may have been adjusted; this should be clearly communicated to all.

- **Prompt decision-making**: Every product is a balance between stakeholder needs and technical feasibility. The Product Owner decides what is built. This requires them to navigate the competing objectives of the stakeholders and technical constraints.

  Prioritization is an essential element of backlog management. The Product Owner should know several prioritization techniques and when to apply them. They should be skilled enough to teach the techniques to the team and the stakeholders.

- **Proactive stakeholder engagement**: There should be regular stakeholder engagement as a group, individually, or some combination of the two. Stakeholders should not need to ask for the Product Owner's time; the Product Owner's responsibility is to ensure recurring events are set up.

  The Product Owner must also be proactive in transparently sharing their decision and the reasons that decision became their choice. Ideally, they will lay out all the positions they have heard from various stakeholders and define their process for choosing as they did. In doing this, they will gain the trust of their stakeholders by being open and honest.

By effectively performing these activities and responsibilities, the Product Owner can ensure the distributed Scrum Team remains aligned with the product vision. Creating and maintaining this alignment, with a value-driven, prioritized backlog, will help the team deliver the value the stakeholders need. The Product Owner, by ensuring ongoing stakeholder engagement, helps the team by ensuring organizational alignment behind their efforts.

Working as a distributed Scrum Team member

Distributed Scrum Team members are responsible for delivering the increments of a product with high quality every Sprint. For distributed teams, additional challenges are caused by time zones and cultural differences. Each team member must proactively address their ways of working to ensure the greatest results for the team and the product. Furthermore, each team member must be skilled in their respective technical disciplines and be willing to improve their skills by learning other disciplines that are being implemented in the team.

Self-management

Self-management is the ability to manage your time and work. It includes additional skills, such as self-organization, motivation, and monitoring. It also includes the ability to collaborate effectively, especially across time zones. Flexibility and adaptability are musts on distributed teams.

Individual team members are also expected to take full ownership of their tasks. They should be taking tasks from the Sprint Backlog without prompting and be willing to ask for help when they need it. Each team member is aware of the Sprint timebox, so they need to manage their workload effectively to deliver within that timebox.

Finally, there is a default expectation that each team member will deliver the highest quality deliverables possible. Being accountable for the quality of your work is essential in distributed environments, where there may be hours-long delays between coding and code reviews. Therefore, each person must ensure they are writing clean code that meets organizational standards and has conducted thorough testing on their own.

Technical capabilities

Every Scrum Team has a unique product that exists in a unique ecosystem and requires a collection of unique skills to create and maintain. All team members are expected to come to the team with a base skillset that will help deliver a product incrementally.

The team member needs to stay up to date and current with their skills in their area of specialty. Additionally, they need to stay abreast of the technologies being used or introduced into the environment. Tracking industry trends is also helpful to maintain and update your skills proactively.

Finally, a mindset of continuous learning and self-improvement will help distributed team members set an example for others on the team regarding how to increase their skills and proficiency. An openness and willingness to learn the other skills that are required for product delivery will help immensely. As individuals become cross-skilled or learn other disciplines, the team can accelerate and deliver work efficiently.

Cross-functional collaboration

Collaboration among developers, designers, testers, and other roles is critical to the team's success. Each team member must be willing to work with their fellows from other disciplines to ensure proper work coordination is taking place. Team distribution can make this active collaboration challenging, and all involved will need to be flexible and willing to adjust their schedule to ensure this takes place.

Additionally, cross-skilling with others on the team enables team members to contribute to all aspects of product development. This means team members are regularly expected to write and review code, test, provide feedback, and pair program to learn new skills.

Outcomes of a skilled distributed Scrum Team member

When a distributed team member is performing their role effectively, the results will be evident. To be, or to assess the ability of, an excellent distributed team member, look for these outcomes:

- **Proactive communication and coordination**: Regularly updating the team on their progress, sharing learnings, and asking for help will indicate that the team member is fully engaged in the work and focused on the product increment.

  Using collaboration tools proficiently while following the guidelines the team has established will ensure the team member is collaborating as effectively as possible.

- **High-quality work and accountability**: Delivering high-quality work consistently is an excellent indicator of both technical skill and attention to testing and details. Thoroughly self-testing code is expected, as is seeking feedback from code reviewers to ensure self-improvement.

  Taking responsibility for tasks from start to finish, meeting deadlines, and addressing any issues that arise are all part of the ownership that is expected from all team members.

- **Active engagement**: In distributed teams, it is challenging to foster a team culture. Actively participating in team activities, from Scrum events and discussions to team lunches, is expected to help build comradeship.

  Supporting peer team members is also expected to occur. This can take the form of helping someone solve a problem or simply providing feedback when needed. This will help build trust within the team.

- **Continuous improvement**: Self-improvement and ongoing skill enhancement fall within the category of continuous improvement. Scrum Team members seek to improve themselves as much as they seek to improve their products and processes.

Active participation in Scrum Retrospectives is essential to helping facilitate healthy Scrum events and artifacts. All team members are expected to share their feedback and ideas on ways to improve.

By performing these responsibilities effectively, along with maintaining and improving their skills, team members in a distributed team help ensure success. These behaviors will foster collaboration, quality deliverables, and high performance.

Learning distributed cross-functional collaboration

Effective cross-functional collaboration in a distributed Scrum Team involves overcoming several challenges related to communication, coordination, and cultural differences. Addressing these is essential for the team to function as a seamless whole and deliver high-quality products.

Coordination across time zones

To ensure that everyone is working together efficiently, regularly speaking to each other in real time is essential. Furthermore, it reduces the likelihood of miscommunication:

- **Schedule meetings to accommodate different time zones**: One of the main challenges in distributed teams is finding appropriate times for meetings. This involves using tools such as World Time Buddy or Microsoft Scheduling Assistance to identify overlapping work hours and schedule important meetings during these times.

- **Use asynchronous communication effectively**: For teams spread across various time zones, relying on asynchronous communication is crucial. This includes using tools such as Slack, Teams, Confluence, and email to share updates and documents that team members can access and respond to at their convenience.

Cultural differences

Cultural misunderstandings, such as differences in work ethics or expectations, can cause difficulty within the team. Improving cultural awareness is critical:

- **Build cultural awareness and sensitivity**: Understanding and respecting cultural differences can enhance collaboration and reduce misunderstandings. This involves providing cultural sensitivity training and encouraging open discussions about cultural norms and preferences.

- **Encourage inclusive communication**: Ensure that all team members feel comfortable contributing to discussions, regardless of their location or background. This includes using inclusive language and being mindful of different communication styles.

Facilitation in distributed teams

The role of facilitation is crucial in distributed teams to ensure that meetings are productive and that all team members can participate fully.

Tips to facilitate meetings

It is the Scrum Master who facilitates most Scrum events. Regardless of who is responsible for this effort, the best practices for successful facilitation remain the same. Here are the most important actions you can take:

- **Lead virtual meetings**: Effective virtual meetings require clear agendas, defined roles (e.g., facilitator, note-taker), and the use of collaboration tools such as Zoom, Miro, or Google Meet. Setting ground rules for participation, such as muting when not speaking and using hand-raise features, can also help. Define these things before the meeting begins so that everyone is prepared.

- **Engage participants**: Use interactive tools such as polls, breakout rooms, and collaborative documents to keep participants engaged and encourage active participation through questions, discussions, and feedback loops.

Encourage participation

It can be argued that unless everyone participates actively in a meeting, it is unsuccessful. A skilled facilitator will have strategies to ensure that everyone in attendance is an active participant:

- **Ensure all voices are heard**: Actively solicit input from all team members, especially those who may be less vocal. This can be achieved through round-robin discussions, anonymous surveys, and direct invitations to contribute.
- **Techniques to foster active involvement**: Implement techniques such as brainstorming sessions, icebreakers, and team-building activities to foster a sense of belonging and encourage active involvement.

Vision-setting in a distributed environment

Setting and maintaining a clear product vision is vital for keeping a distributed team aligned and motivated.

Communicate the vision

The Product Owner must regularly share the product vision through virtual town halls, vision boards, and video messages from leadership. Ensure that the vision is accessible and well-understood by all team members.

Reinforce the vision through daily Scrums, Sprint Planning, and Retrospective events. Use visual aids and documentation to keep the vision front and center.

Maintain focus on the vision

Keep the team aligned with the vision during Sprints by revisiting it during daily Scrums, Sprint Reviews, and planning sessions. This will ensure that the team's work aligns with the overarching goals.

Adjust the vision based on feedback and changing requirements. The Product Owner must remain open to feedback from the team and stakeholders. They must be willing to adjust their vision as needed. This involves maintaining flexibility while keeping the core objectives intact.

Self-management in distributed teams

Self-management is a key aspect of a successful distributed Scrum Team, where team members take responsibility for their tasks and collaborate effectively.

Empower team members

Encouraging autonomy and accountability is important. Trust team members to manage their work and make decisions. This includes providing the necessary tools and resources, setting clear expectations, and recognizing individual contributions.

Provide the necessary resources and support. Ensure that team members have access to the tools, training, and support they need to perform their tasks effectively. This includes technical resources, training, and access to mentors or coaches.

Monitor and adjust

Use tools such as JIRA, Trello, or Asana to track tasks and monitor progress. Implement daily Scrums and status updates to keep everyone informed and address any issues promptly.

You must also be flexible and responsive to changes in the product or team dynamics. Encourage a culture of continuous improvement where team members can suggest and implement changes to enhance productivity and collaboration without having to wait for a formal Retrospective event.

Outcomes of healthy, distributed cross-functional collaboration

A distributed Scrum Team that excels in cross-functional collaboration would demonstrate a variety of characteristics and outcomes. Let's take a look.

Clear communication and coordination

As a distributed team, you will have more than one communication channel at your disposal; using them wisely requires forethought:

- **Seamless use of communication tools**: Team members use a variety of communication tools effectively, ensuring that everyone is informed and engaged. Meetings are well-organized, productive, and inclusive of all time zones and locations.

- **Effective asynchronous communication**: Information is shared clearly and promptly through asynchronous channels, allowing team members to stay updated and contribute regardless of their time zone.

Strong cultural sensitivity and inclusivity

As the leader of a team that spans the globe, you must lead by example when it comes to cultural sensitivity. Bridging communication differences requires you to model the following behaviors:

- **Cultural awareness**: The team demonstrates high cultural sensitivity, respecting and valuing diverse perspectives. Team members are aware of cultural differences and adapt their communication and collaboration styles accordingly.

- **Inclusive practices**: All team members feel valued and included, with opportunities to contribute and participate in discussions. The team fosters a supportive and inclusive environment.

Effective facilitation and engagement

The benefits of these practices are numerous. When you elevate your facilitation skills, you will generate freedom within the team to explore complex topics in safety. Additionally, you can expect the following:

- **Productive meetings**: Meetings are engaging and productive, with clear agendas and active participation from all team members. The team uses interactive tools and techniques to maintain engagement.

- **Active involvement**: Team members are actively involved in discussions and decision-making processes, contributing their expertise and insights. The team values and encourages diverse viewpoints.

Consistent vision and alignment

When you communicate the vision for your product effectively and consistently, you create a team that is productive and fully focused on turning their aspirations into tangible outcomes:

- **Clear and communicated vision**: The product vision is clearly communicated and reinforced regularly, ensuring that all team members understand and align with it. The vision guides the team's work and decisions.

- **Adaptability to feedback**: The team is responsive to feedback and willing to adjust the vision as needed while maintaining focus on core objectives. This flexibility helps the team stay aligned with changing requirements and stakeholder needs.

High level of self-management

Due to their consistent focus on the desired outcome, the team will need less direction and be able to manage themselves and their work delivery:

- **Autonomy and accountability**: Team members take ownership of their tasks and are accountable for their work. They manage their time effectively and collaborate proactively to achieve team goals.

- **Continuous improvement**: The team embraces a culture of continuous improvement, regularly reflecting on performance and implementing changes to enhance productivity and collaboration. Feedback is valued and used to drive improvements.

By mastering these aspects of distributed cross-functional collaboration, a Scrum Team can overcome the challenges of working remotely, maintain strong relationships, and deliver high-quality products efficiently.

Summary

The strength of Scrum comes from its simplicity. An essential element of that simplicity is the limited number of roles on the Scrum Team. Remember, the Scrum Team includes the Product Owner, Scrum Master, and Development Team. The effectiveness these three roles bring to the team depends on the clarity of the roles and the responsibilities that lie within them.

In this chapter, we closely examined each of the three Scrum roles and studied the skills and outcomes needed to excel in these roles. As each member of your distributed Scrum Team masters each of these key skills, you will get the high-quality product outcomes you are looking for. In the next chapter, we will address the steps you must take to ensure your distributed Scrum Team has all the tools they need to drive their success.

4

Setting Up for Remote Scrum Success

A profound transformation of the working landscape has happened in the recent years. Remote work has become a significant part of how teams operate across industries. At the same time, organizations have increasingly adopted Agile and Scrum frameworks; the challenge is to maintain the integrity of the frameworks in a remote setting.

This chapter is about guiding you through setting up your remote Scrum Team for success. We will explore crucial elements that ensure a team's success and ability to thrive, including choosing tools for seamless communication and establishing clear working agreements. Additionally, we will explore the importance of creating a productive home office environment and discuss time management strategies.

The following topics have been covered in this chapter:

- Choosing the right tools for remote collaboration
- Establishing working agreements
- Creating a productive home office environment
- Time management for remote teams

Choosing the right tools for remote collaboration

Scrum demands transparency, inspection, and adaptation from teams that use it. The roles in Scrum (*Product Owner*, *Scrum Master*, and *Development Team*) need to continually communicate requirements, process notes, and design ideas with each other. If care is not taken in selecting tools with their specific functional needs in mind, your remote team cannot succeed.

The right toolset will not solve all the problems your team may face, but it can mitigate some risks before they become issues. Proper tooling makes it easier to build good, healthy habits around regular communication, thus minimizing communication barriers time and distance create. When you take the time and put thought into setting up your distributed teams, you will get greater flexibility in your talent pool and the potential for higher productivity.

Evaluating technology needs

Selecting the right tools is essential to ensuring that tasks are planned and completed efficiently. They also help ensure that the team remains aligned on Sprint and release goals throughout the Sprint. These tools can also enhance the team's flexibility and help them work more efficiently.

Understanding team requirements

As you go through the tool selection process, you must consider each of the Scrum roles individually and their unique perspectives on what will serve them best:

- **Product Owner**: The Product Owner will be most concerned with ensuring the Product Backlog is easy to create, prioritize, and manage. It needs to have a user interface where it is simple to link to external documents and hold notes regarding the story's requirements. Some capabilities for the Product Owner could include product planning and release planning. They may also want to use the tool to measure the release burndown using a chart.

- **Scrum Master**: The Scrum Master will wish for a work tracking tool that is simple for everyone to use and powerful enough to generate key Scrum metrics. There needs to be a simple user interface where the team members can take notes on their work and tag other team members for action if needed. Key metrics for the Scrum Master could include the Sprint Burndown chart, the Commit to Complete Ratio, and the Number of Defects found in Testing, among others.

- **Development Team**: The Development Team will vary based on the type of work they do. For example, a software Development Team will be most interested in a work management tool that integrates with their code management tool. They may be interested in tracking design sessions and code review results.

The only way to know what will serve your team best is to ask them. If possible, include them in the entire technology evaluation process. It can be a useful way to ensure their buy-in on the technology stack that is implemented.

A final area of consideration is that of integration and scalability. Your team is a member of the organizational ecosystem, so whichever tool(s) you choose must be integrated into that ecosystem. Please be sure to include your technical infrastructure experts as part of your selection process.

Additionally, be sure to confirm the scalability of your tools; they need to be able to grow to support access for your team's key stakeholders to see what work is happening. Agile frameworks and Scrum welcome stakeholder involvement in the process. This business and technology collaboration makes Scrum successful; ensure your tools support this aspect of Scrum, too.

Selecting essential tools

For every Scrum Team searching for tools, there are three broad categories that will need to be covered. Those categories are communication and collaboration, project management, and code management. Each should be considered separately before seeking overlaps to reduce the budget and technical costs of adoption. You are seeking best-in-class, if possible, to ensure the highest likelihood of distributed team success:

- **Communication and collaboration tools**: This is a broad category of tools and encompasses a few subcategories:

  - Video conferencing, screen sharing, and recording

  - Direct messaging and group chats

  - Document co-editing and sharing

  - Visual collaboration tools and digital whiteboarding

  - Interactive dashboards for progress tracking

  - Popular options in this category include Slack, Teams, Zoom, Mural, and Miro

- **Project management tools**: These tools are for organizing the body of all work the team could deliver; there are several functions for you to assess:

  - Backlog management for user stories, tasks, and bugs

  - Prioritization techniques such as Kano and MoSCoW

  - Sprint Planning

  - Metrics generation and dashboards

  - Popular options include Jira, Trello, and Asana

- **Code management tools**: Developers will need an integrated set of tools to manage development and testing activities. Here, you need to assess the following:

  - Code automation, including deployment tools such as Jenkins or AWS CodeDeploy

  - Source code management, including tools such as GitHub and Bitbucket

  - Code review tools are built into code management tools such as GitHub and Bitbucket

  - Testing, including unit, integration, and system testing tools such as Katalon or Selenium

As you journey through tool evaluation and selection, you have an opportunity to ensure that your team begins with all the right tools to help them successfully execute distributed Scrum. These tools are not all they need to succeed, though; they also need to learn how to use the tools appropriately and agree as a unit on what that must look like. This is where our next section will help you form a healthy team unit.

Establishing working agreements

When a team initially forms, this is one of the most important first steps to take. Team working agreements are also known as a team charter or their operating principles. These are agreements all team members define and agree upon to ensure they are working as effectively as possible:

- **Roles and responsibilities**: Working agreements often stipulate the roles of teams to ensure there is no overlap of accountability. Also often included are some guidelines for distributing work according to team members' strengths and weaknesses. Finally, it is a good idea to call out how the team will handle cross-skilling so that there are no **single points of failure** (SPOFs) on the team.

- **Communication protocols**: These agreements are about what tools to use for which types of communication, including guidelines for email, chat, and video. These are also used to establish cadences for daily Scrum, Sprint Planning, and Retrospectives. You can also establish a frequency for informal check-ins and team-building activities.

- **Defining work processes**: Often, teams will establish what their working hours are in their time zone to make it easy for their colleagues to reach them. You may also establish protocols for expected response times to chats, emails, and missed calls. Additionally, your agreement should include adjustments the team will make to accommodate the various time zones represented on the team. Care should be taken that all zones are equally "inconvenienced" by the team's distribution.

- **Feedback and continuous improvement**: In this area, the team needs to define how they will share feedback with each other beyond the team Retrospective. For example, your team may determine that constructive feedback will only be given over a video call and in private, while positive feedback can be given at any time over any medium.

- **Building a team culture**: Your team agreements should formalize expectations about team-building activities and the absolute requirement that all participate. Finally, your agreement should outline ways in which team members commit to creating an inclusive environment to ensure all voices are heard and adopting cultural sensitivity in communications.

You will host a team agreement definition meeting. It is recommended that you prepare the team by explaining what the agreements are and why they are important. Provide your team members with "homework" to complete before the meeting. An interesting technique is to ask them to come to the meeting with details about the best team they were ever a member of and why. This will ensure team members have the right frame of mind to begin defining what will be satisfying to them in this team.

As you facilitate this meeting, you may recognize you can only control the tools the team uses and how they work together. Some things outside of work are distractions you cannot control. You can, at least, make recommendations to minimize those distractions by helping guide their home office choices; this is where our next section can help you.

Creating a productive home office environment

When working in an office environment, there are constant distractions – people walking by, stopping by to chat, and asking questions. In a remote work environment, the office is your home, and the potential for distraction is much greater. In this section, we will explore recommendations you could make to team members to ensure their home office is conducive to efficiency and effectiveness while minimizing distractions.

Optimizing physical workspace

First, consider how best to optimize your physical workspace. Ideally, the office should be a dedicated space for your team members. It should be available for their work and be away from other people who may be home while they are working. Having a door that closes is also an important method to minimize distractions.

There are ergonomic desks and chairs that team members should consider. Many people get up from their desks less often when working from home, making furniture comfort of utmost importance. Keyboard and mouse ergonomics are also essential and should be considered as viable options. Additionally, the placement of these devices needs to be designed for the specific person. Considering this, it is best to ensure their equipment is ideally suited to their body type. For more information, check out this article: `https://www.posturite.co.uk/blog/`.

A final consideration few recognize is that of lighting. When optimizing your physical workspace, consider the type and amount of lighting in your home office. Natural light is best overall for well-being and productivity. Supplement with artificial lighting that shares the same spectrum as natural light. Doing this simple thing can help your team members boost their output and their efficiency.

Minimizing distractions

Minimizing distractions goes well beyond the privacy and seclusion of your home office space. In our modern world of cell phones and social media, we carry our distractions with us everywhere we go. When working from home, boundaries between work and personal space and time can become blurred.

Begin by considering what your primary distractors are. For example, some people cannot work if their desk is messy. If this is your distraction, you will need to commit to yourself that you will tidy your desk at the end of each day. Other common distractions can include pets, household members, neighbors, or even household chores. Consider what you will do to minimize or remove these distractions.

Next on our list of distractions is our digital devices. These include our cell phones, apps, and social media notifications, as well as emails and pings from our team members on chat at work. One strategy is to silence your devices and apps for specific time periods while you focus on work.

To avoid becoming overwhelmed, silence things for 1 hour, check them, address anything urgent, and silence them again. The bonus to this strategy is that you can link this as a trigger to get up out of your chair, step away from your desk, and move for a little while.

Technological setup

Beyond the toolset that you carefully chose for the success of your team, the team is also at the mercy of team members' at-home technical infrastructure. In these times of frequent remote work, your organization may already have guidelines and best practices for employees to follow. You will also want to follow up individually with each person to ensure they are abiding by those guidelines.

You may be wondering about the questions to ask and follow up regarding concerns with internet connectivity. Issues associated with connectivity are particularly important given that the team is distributed. Your team members need to ensure they have stable and consistent internet connectivity and that their internet speed is sufficient for the highly technical work they will do for your team. You can establish minimum speed and uptime requirements to guide your team in selecting an appropriate internet carrier.

Explore with your team members their backup plan for unexpected downtime or lag. One option in this arena includes mobile hotspots. Another option is to go to a local library with free, albeit slow, internet connectivity.

Finally, be sure to address hardware and software optimization when your organization provides equipment for team members. Ensure tools and applications are optimized for remote work. Offer backup power solutions to employees, such as **uninterruptible power supply** (UPS) systems, if you can. Make sure that the software is set up to automatically update with enhancements and security patches to ensure security and performance.

One final note on automating software updates. This is a wonderful idea and will ensure the security and integrity of the hardware and software your team uses. Please be sure to request a notification be sent to employees at least 24 hours before the patching and updates occur so that they can leave their device powered up or, alternately, boot their machine early so as not to impact their workday. It can be frustrating, as a remote worker, to log on in the morning and undergo a 30-minute delay for patches and updates to apply and a reboot to occur.

As you guide your team members toward following these best practices for creating a productive home office environment, you will reap rewards as a team. Focus, clarity, efficiency, and productivity result from considering all these aspects of working remotely. Addressing them at the beginning will save everyone time.

Time management for remote teams

Time management is the process of organizing and planning how you will divide your time across the commitments you have made in Sprint Planning. In a distributed environment, there is no one in person to hold you to account for completing your work. Remote team members are, therefore, self-managed. That makes this topic an essential one to cover on every distributed Scrum Team:

- **Setting clear goals and objectives**: Scrum itself helps in this regard because each Sprint has a defined Sprint Goal. Every team member's work is aligned with that goal and time-boxed.

- **Using time management tools**: Use scheduling tools such as calendars or timers to block work time. Managing time zones becomes much easier when using a tool such as World Time Buddy to help schedule meetings and keep track of your team members' schedules.

- **Synchronizing across time zones**: Identify and leverage overlapping work hours so that you can hold synchronous activities. This is especially helpful for Scrum events, team-building activities, and design meetings.

- **Flexible work hours**: Establish guidelines for what flexible work hours look like in your team. This is a great subject for your team's working agreements. If there are hours during which everyone should be online, call them out and make them required. Flexibility can be applied to other working windows.

- **Recognizing signs of burnout**: Everyone has limits to what they can accomplish. Watch for signs of burnout in your team members. You will see decreased productivity, increased errors, and disengagement. You will also see emotional signs such as anxiety, stress, and irritability. When you see these, act by encouraging open dialogue, holding regular check-ins, and even encouraging team members to take some time away from work.

- **Promoting work-life balance**: Encourage team members to step away from their desks several times a day to move around and disengage from their computers. These regular breaks will help them maintain their well-being. It will also ensure you continue to see the quality and productivity in them that you have come to expect.

The benefits of these efforts are clear: improved project outcomes, enhanced team cohesion, and a more engaged and satisfied workforce. However, the journey to remote Scrum success is ongoing. Continuous feedback and adaptation are crucial to addressing new challenges and seizing emerging opportunities in a dynamic work environment.

Summary

Successfully transitioning to remote Scrum requires more than just adapting to a new way of working; it demands thoughtful planning, deliberate action, and continuous improvement. By carefully selecting the right tools for communication and collaboration, establishing clear and actionable working agreements, creating a productive home office environment, and mastering time management, Scrum Teams can overcome challenges posed by remote work and unlock new levels of productivity and satisfaction.

In our next chapter, we will study the need for healthy Scrum Teams to bring distributed teams to life. Even with clear roles and responsibilities and a perfect home office environment, more is needed. You need to create an environment that fosters team cohesion. Only with this in place will the fruits of your labors around roles, responsibilities, tools, and office appear.

Part 2:
Team Building and Cohesion

One of the primary drivers behind Scrum is the solid foundation of the Scrum Team. All Scrum Teams must be cohesive and collaborate closely to succeed; this is particularly challenging for remote teams. This part covers strategies for recruiting, onboarding, and integrating team members across distances. The chapters in this part provide actionable advice on creating an atmosphere of trust with transparency and managing performance remotely.

This part has the following chapters:

Chapter 5, Recruiting and Forming a Distributed Scrum Team

Chapter 6, Cultivating a Strong Remote Culture

Chapter 7, Effective Communication and Working Agreements

Chapter 8, Managing Performance and Motivation

5

Recruiting and Forming a Distributed Scrum Team

The dramatic shift from in-person work to remote work has demanded a change in how Scrum Teams are formed and managed. Distributed Scrum Teams, spread across various geographies, bring unique challenges and opportunities. This chapter explores the process of recruiting and forming a distributed Scrum Team, emphasizing the critical skills and strategies needed for success. The focus is on identifying the right talent, implementing effective onboarding processes, fostering a culture of inclusivity, and setting clear expectations and goals.

In this chapter, we're going to cover the following main topics:

- Identifying skills for distributed Scrum Team roles
- Effective remote onboarding processes
- Building an inclusive team culture
- Setting expectations and goals

Identifying skills for distributed Scrum Team roles

On every Scrum Team are three key roles: the **Product Owner**, the **Scrum Master**, and the **Development Team**. For each role, you will evaluate the candidates on both quantifiable, job-specific competencies and soft skills. One can argue that the hard skills can be taught, but the soft skills are difficult to teach. As you explore this section, consider how you might balance the hard skills and the soft skills in evaluating your candidates.

Seeking soft skills for all roles

Soft skills, simply stated, are how well you work with others. Regardless of an individual's technical competency in their role, without the right soft skills, they will be difficult to work with and could become an insurmountable obstacle to team success. Since a healthy team is the foundation of successful Scrum, we can state that soft skills among the team members are the foundation of hiring the right talent for your team. With so much riding on these soft skills, we will examine seven key soft skills in turn.

Teamwork

Working effectively as a team results in more productive teams that meet their deadlines. Their relationships with each other are strong, and knowledge is shared openly. Individuals who excel at teamwork will achieve personal goals and support their team members in doing the same.

Individuals with strong teamwork skills will keep their team's objectives in mind as well as understand how their own contributions and commitments relate to the big picture. These individuals are supportive of their peers, communicate regularly, and are active listeners.

If a candidate lacks depth in the teamwork area or is new to working in a team environment, you can deepen these skills as part of your work, as a leader, on team building. Establishing working agreements (see *Chapter 7*) will help frame the kind of teamwork expected.

Some questions to consider asking candidates regarding this soft skill are as follows:

- Can you please provide an example of your teamwork skills?
- How do you handle a team situation in which something went wrong?
- What is your biggest contribution to your teams?

Problem-solving

Hurdles always arise for all teams, no matter how carefully we have established the working environment. *When hurdles do appear, you need to trust that the members of your team will remain calm and focused and will arrive at solutions.*

Individuals who are effective problem-solvers will immediately act by trying to understand the situation from all angles. They will research options, understand the complexities, and offer more than one possible solution. They will draw on their critical thinking skills to brainstorm viable solutions and make recommendations.

An effective way to build this skill among your team members is to encourage them to research and solve problems independently. Holding design sessions or issue-resolution meetings can help steer the team toward better problem-solving and self-organization.

For this soft skill, there are some options to consider:

- Use situational or behavioral questions such as "Describe a time when you faced an unexpected challenge at work".

- Provide a case study or simulation for them to solve

- Use aptitude tests

Communication

This is the soft skill we are all most familiar with, and for good reason. Excellent communication means that you can actively listen, understand varying perspectives, and be able to share your own ideas effectively. Not everyone has this skill, and its necessity on your team, in every role, is critical.

Strong communicators know their audience, use clear, concise language, and are empathetic to those who are present. They manage their body language and tone of voice to match their message.

You can identify candidates with excellent communication skills by carefully observing their responses to your interview questions. Enhancement of communication skills will be part of the ongoing team dynamic. Working agreements can set a baseline understanding for communication within the team, and creating feedback avenues for team members will help them enhance their communication skills.

Adaptability

Not everyone can cope with change in a positive way and successfully adapt to whatever comes along. Adaptability is crucial for members of a Scrum Team, where changing requirements are welcomed.

Adaptable individuals make sure they completely understand changes that are coming and keep an open mind. They seek opportunities in the change coming and plan the practical steps to adopt the change. These individuals are willing to step outside their comfort zones and build new habits. As the team leader, you will help individuals grow their adaptability by observing them and offering feedback. Criticism is not the objective, rather, your goal is to coach them by offering alternative reactions and helping them find a way to become more comfortable with change.

You can identify adaptable individuals in an interview assessment with the following questions:

- How do you handle changes in your work environment or job responsibilities?

- Describe a time you had to adjust your approach to complete a task

Critical thinking

Individuals with strong critical thinking skills effectively analyze information and weigh the pros and cons of myriad options. Assessing this skill for your Scrum Team means you are seeking individuals who can quickly assimilate information around complex problems and efficiently make recommendations.

As you encourage the team toward self-organization, you will also be encouraging their critical thinking skills. As they solve problems and gain confidence in their own wisdom, they will begin to follow the path of alternative options and possible outcomes. This is the heart of critical thinking.

Some questions to help you identify a candidate with strong critical thinking skills are as follows:

- Walk me through a decision or recommendation you made that involved weighing different options and their possible consequences
- Tell me about a time you had to convince your boss or a team member to use an alternative approach to solve a problem

Time management

Effectively managing your time enables you to take control of your day and minimize the stress of not knowing how to prioritize your tasks. Individuals on your Scrum Team must be able to independently allocate their work across all the hours of the day and all the days of the Scrum.

Individuals who excel at this skill can quickly and effectively differentiate between what is urgent and what is not. They then stay committed to these priorities while remaining flexible if priorities shift.

Team members will improve their time management skills as you help them prioritize their tasks. Help them to see the dependencies within the work of the team and then ask them how best to prioritize to minimize disruptions to the flow of work. Additionally, be sure to encourage them to fully finish one thing at a time and avoid multitasking.

When assessing for time management skills, you can use questions such as these:

- How do you prioritize your work each day?
- What tools or techniques do you use to manage your time effectively?

Interpersonal skills

These skills are the ones that enable an individual to build relationships and communicate well with others. These are the behaviors used every day to interact with others, both on teams and in mundane situations such as buying groceries.

These skills will underpin all the activities on your team and must be carefully assessed. Those with strong interpersonal skills are active listeners and have high emotional intelligence. They can resolve conflicts without assistance and maintain mutually beneficial working relationships.

You can help your team members grow their interpersonal skills by encouraging them to give and receive feedback in appropriate ways. With the help of your **human resources (HR)** representative, you can present training and guidance on active listening, empathy, and feedback. You can also model these skills by using them with everyone on the team.

Use questions such as these to evaluate a candidate's interpersonal skills:

- Tell me about the most challenging individual with whom you have ever interacted and how you worked together

- Describe a time when you came into conflict with a team member and how you resolved the conflict

Focusing on soft skills ensures you can form a team that can advance in cohesion and performance. Simply stated, soft skills are how well you work with others. With your care and attention to these details, you will ensure that your distributed team has all the foundational elements needed to succeed.

Balancing vision and drive: Product Owner

The Product Owner (PO) is responsible for managing the Product Backlog (PB). This includes ensuring it is updated as per priority. Business changes daily, so it is only logical that the PO should also reflect those changes in the backlog daily. In addition to the skills listed previously, there are more skills to seek in the person filling this role. One key aspect of this hard skill is the related soft skill of negotiation.

Negotiation is an essential skill for the PO to possess. It is important to note that the PO is not necessarily negotiating with an end in mind beyond delivering the best product possible. POs are negotiating to ensure the interests of all stakeholders are heard, understood, and considered as the backlog is prioritized.

The PO needs to balance the perspectives of all the key stakeholders invested in your product. Using these conversations and requirement-gathering sessions, they are actively listening to the needs and root causes behind the needs to ensure that the root causes are addressed effectively. They are further envisioning downstream impacts of each stakeholder's requests to ensure they do not conflict with other desired outcomes.

For the PO, the desired outcome is always the best possible product, launched as quickly as possible, and with the highest level of quality. Their negotiation skills, along with active listening, can build robust stakeholder relationships. These relationships are the foundation for ongoing collaboration, support when requesting additional resources, and alignment with company objectives.

Facilitating remotely: Scrum Master

As the person responsible for enabling Scrum success, the **Scrum Master** (**SM**) needs additional skills as well. Foremost among these skills is the skill of facilitation itself. Facilitation is far more than simply scheduling events and ensuring they are held. It also encompasses supporting the team through conflict and ensuring there is enough lightweight structure to ensure all voices are being heard and event objectives are met efficiently.

Lyssa Adkins, author and Agile Coach, said it best: *"A Scrum Master should facilitate by creating a "container" for the team to fill up with their ideas and innovations. The container, often a set of agenda questions or some other lightweight (and flexible) structure, gives the team just enough of a frame to stay on their purpose and promotes an environment for richer interaction, a place where fantastic ideas can be heard. The coach creates the container; the team creates the content."*

The event "container" is collectively the time and venue, along with a stated objective. Having an agenda is one way to structure the event. Another lightweight way is to state the objective of the event and include a series of questions to trigger conversation.

For example, perhaps a team member is blocked on one of their work items. If there is more than one approach to solving this problem, the SM will gather the team together for a brief solutioning session. The agenda may simply consist of the objective to decide upon a design approach, an overview of the issue, and a list of questions to consider, such as "What will be most sustainable?", "Which option will incur the least technical debt?" and "Which option will best suit the architectural direction of the organization?"

Within this event container, the team explores the topics and issues at hand. If you are lucky, there will be some level of amicable conflict within the team about the best next steps. This is a positive occurrence and is managed by a skilled facilitator. Conflicts and disagreements on approach will result in a more robust product design. A skilled SM will know when to step in to keep the disagreement productive. This is a crucial soft skill learned in the trenches and can rarely be taught, so it is important to seek this level of facilitation skill in your interviewing process.

Finally, removing impediments is another essential aspect of the SM role. Often, team members do not realize they are blocked because they are so close to the work. The SM, on the other hand, has just enough distance and maintains the big-picture view such that impediments are more evident to them.

One advantage of the Daily Scrum is that you can receive early clues to problems that may be bubbling just under the surface. Some key words to listen for are "unsure," "waiting," "unusual situation/result," and so on. These can be clues that something is amiss for the team member. The SM will step in with some post-Scrum questions to dig deeper and search for root causes. Root causes may be communication breakdowns, unrealized expectations, time zone challenges, and technical issues. The skilled SM will have a toolkit from which to pull diverse options to alleviate and remediate root causes so progress can continue to be made.

Delivering sustainably: Development Team

In addition to the core skills already covered for all team members, the Developers need to be assessed for their technical skills. Any team member doing the work of delivering the product is considered a "Developer" in terms of Scrum. Typical assessments of technical skills include requests for the interviewee to solve a coding problem or to provide a sample test case for a defined user story.

Assessing the willingness and experience of team members to write code collaboratively and use tools that facilitate asynchronous communication is an element to keep in mind. Seeing specific experience with platforms such as GitHub and GitLab can help you with your assessment of their skills.

In a distributed environment, **continuous integration/continuous delivery (CI/CD)** is critical to ensure that the team's work is integrated into a cohesive whole regularly. In this type of environment, the code base is likely to be developed in parallel around the clock based on the locations of the team members. Experience with CI/CD and automated testing can help maintain code quality and ensure that no changes are accidentally overwritten. Seeking these skills will help your team immensely.

There are essential skills you will need to seek as you build your team. Consult with other remote teams in your organization to learn what tools, techniques, and interview questions worked well for them. Finally, consult with your HR department to learn what online skill assessment tools are being used.

Many HR departments are investigating and implementing skill assessment tools that can be used for both hard and soft skills. They are not only applicable to the hiring process, but can also be used continuously to grow team members' skills throughout their careers with your team. Examples of this type of tool are Skillable and Vervoe.

The entire organization wants you and your team to succeed with the right team members. Make sure you are asking for support along the way.

In the next section, we will examine how these carefully selected individuals can join your team effectively and get up to speed as quickly as possible.

Onboarding remote workers

Onboarding is far more than simply providing a laptop and access; it's the journey of making them feel welcomed, supported, and like the valued asset you were seeking. Considering this, you must begin your onboarding work well in advance of the team member's first day on the job.

In this section, we're going to explore key onboarding activities that could increase retention and reduce turnover. These steps will also set the foundation for their role and how they fit into the larger organization. Investing care and attention early in someone's journey with you will pay dividends for years to come.

Pre-onboarding preparation

A week or more in advance of your new team member's arrival, your first task will be to think through their onboarding plan. You will need to tailor this plan to the individual, their role, and their time zone.

In this stage of onboarding, you will be focused on ensuring that all the essentials are ready for them on day one. You will process all the new hire paperwork and request equipment for them. The equipment itself may be a multi-step process wherein you need to define exactly which hardware and software the employee will need, as well as details for delivery. At the same time, you will be completing paperwork to ensure the new team member has access to all shared documents and design repositories. Finally, if there is a **learning management system** (**LMS**) in your organization, you will define and establish their structured learning path with deadlines for all the courses that are expected to be completed.

Orienting: Day one through week three

Schedule virtual orientation sessions for them and get them set up for introductions with everyone on the team. Engage them immediately in all scheduled Scrum events and team rituals, such as virtual lunches.

Their basic role and associated responsibilities will be assigned to them. Clear pathways for having their questions answered must be defined, as well as an overview of all the ways in which they can provide you with feedback on the orientation and onboarding processes, along with team processes.

In this early stage, you will assign a mentor or team "buddy" to them to help guide them through all team processes, such as entering time and tracking work. This person will be their first stop for all questions they may have about how the team does its work and which tools are used for digital collaboration. Even though they have a "buddy" to work with, make sure you check in with the new employee frequently. This level of attention will ensure they feel welcome and comfortable sharing feedback.

Finally, this is a suitable time to introduce the annual or semi-annual review cycle that exists in your workplace. Be sure to review with them all the criteria on the performance review form and how their specific role and responsibilities will be measured against the general outlines in the documentation. Have examples of various performance levels so there is no ambiguity.

Integrating: month one through month six

At least monthly, review with the employee their performance objectives and progress to date. Also, review their training progress in the LMS and identify any gaps that may exist. They may have already identified areas in which they would like to grow their skills, and you can work through a plan to do so, including a timescale to master current responsibilities first and then enrich their skills.

Often, around month three or four, you may opt to hold an informal performance review meeting where you and the employee can take a deeper dive into how things have gone for the employee so far. They will be seeking insights into how their work and team skills are being perceived. For your part, you want to know how to improve your onboarding processes going forward.

When you take the time to properly onboard your new team member, you will set the foundation for success for both the new team member and the whole team. Engagement will be improved across the board, and there will be fewer interruptions to ongoing work and practices.

Building an inclusive team culture

Beyond the technical and communication issues that receive most attention when discussing distributed Scrum Teams, one of the most significant challenges is the blending of diverse cultural, geographic, and professional backgrounds. It requires conscious action to leverage all this diversity into unified strength within the team. In summary, an inclusive team culture is what you are seeking. Once you can harness this diversity and cultural strength, there is little that can stop your team.

There are several actions you can take to encourage this inclusivity. First is to build into your team processes the awareness of *cultural norms and practices*. As a leader, you must begin with yourself and become aware of and respect diverse cultural behaviors. For example, some cultures prefer direct communication while others prefer a more nuanced approach.

Provide your team with cross-cultural training to raise awareness and foster understanding. Your HR department may have standard training materials and courses in the LMS that you can leverage. If possible, it would be a fantastic opportunity for your team members to attend this type of training together and have an open dialogue about what they have learned. Key outcomes from this include an understanding of each other's public holidays, countries, cultures, and work experiences. While this is not a magic bullet, it is an excellent starting point to create empathy and collaboration within the team.

The next step is establishing norms around the use of *inclusive communication practices*. If you work on a technical team, jargon is part of the communication style and shorthand. If jargon is a common language type in use on your team, create a glossary for all team members to access that contains the definition of each jargon word they may encounter. An example of this is the term "Big Data," which refers to large and rapidly growing datasets.

Further, consider adding common colloquialisms to your glossary. A colloquialism is a word or expression used in a certain region that is not widely known or used beyond that region. An example that could make it to your glossary is something such as "low-hanging fruit," which refers to fruit that hangs lowest to the ground and is easiest for people and animals to harvest. In a business context, it means that something is a high-value, low-effort target for work. While many people may be familiar with this colloquialism, many others may not. It is best to add this type of thing to your glossary to ease communication.

Additionally, language inclusivity means everyone is called by their preferred name and referred to by their preferred pronouns. Many companies have explicit preferred name policies and self-identification tools. Consider asking HR to host a brief training session for your team to familiarize them with these policies and expectations.

Once you have built these foundations, it is essential to maintain and grow this understanding and appreciation for the full life cycle of the team. I recommend celebrating all team members' cultural holidays together. Recognize the history and cultural significance of these holidays. It can also be helpful to use these holidays as ongoing anchors for your continued team-building activities.

As you implement these actions to build an inclusive team culture, your team will blossom into an empathetic and collaborative dynamo. Its members will come to each other's assistance and work at odd times to ensure they can come together.

Setting expectations and goals

Setting boundaries and expectations for team members is crucial to their success and, therefore, the success of the whole team and product. Clear role definition and expectations can reduce conflict on the team and ensure each person knows how every role contributes to the Sprint and Product Goals.

As you might imagine, the very first step is to ensure *clarity in role definitions*. While each person, when onboarded, was given their role definition and responsibilities, do not assume everyone on the team has the same understanding. Deepen the understanding of each role across the team and highlight any specialized skills each person has.

Creating a Skill Chart such as this one (`https://www.agilesherpas.com/blog/agile-team-skill-map`) can help with role and specialization definition. It also serves as a tool to highlight areas where cross-training is needed. The following is a sample Skill Chart (or Skill Map).

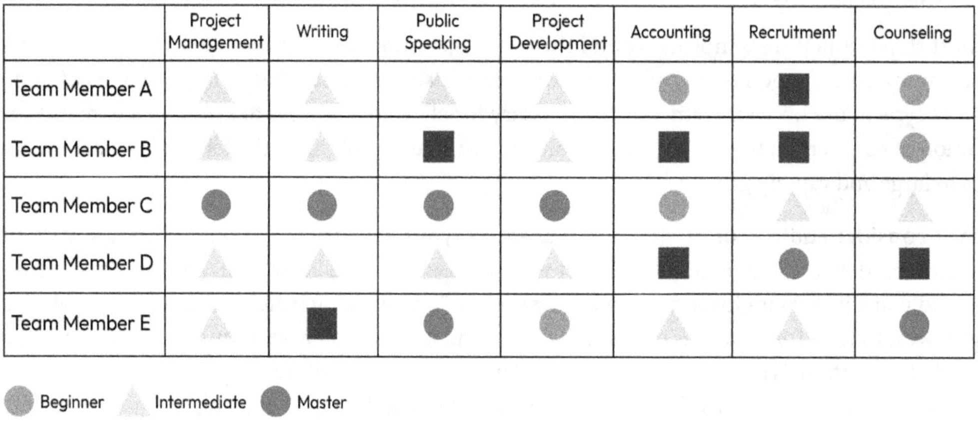

	Project Management	Writing	Public Speaking	Project Development	Accounting	Recruitment	Counseling
Team Member A	Intermediate	Intermediate	Intermediate	Intermediate	Master	Beginner	Master
Team Member B	Intermediate	Intermediate	Beginner	Intermediate	Beginner	Beginner	Master
Team Member C	Master	Master	Master	Master	Master	Intermediate	Intermediate
Team Member D	Intermediate	Intermediate	Intermediate	Intermediate	Beginner	Master	Beginner
Team Member E	Intermediate	Beginner	Master	Master	Intermediate	Intermediate	Master

Beginner · Intermediate · Master

Figure 5.1: Skill Chart

Based on the shapes in use, we can see that accounting skills are an area of risk for this team. There is only one person with intermediate-level skills, and everyone else is either a beginner or has no experience. As the leader of this team, you would work with the team to devise a plan to add bench strength in this skill on the team.

Creating working agreements is the first element of establishing expectations. Also known as "norms" or a "team charter," these establish the baseline rules of engagement within the team. This will establish the values, principles, and behaviors expected of everyone, without exception. This is where you will establish alignment on expectations around communication, collaboration, decision-making, time off, and conflict resolution.

This set of agreements is created collaboratively. Everyone is expected to participate in drafting this document. It is best done in a real-time collaborative session with cameras on and breakout rooms as an option. It is helpful to break the team into pairs or trios and ask them, as sub-groups, to share some of their most effective norms from previous teams on which they have served.

As each sub-group comes back to the main room to share the list of agreements they've developed, it is easy to remove duplicates and identify any gaps. At a minimum, agreements should cover all the items listed previously. Additionally, for widely dispersed teams, it is ideal to agree on meeting times when everyone can come together in real time, regardless of distance.

Now that you have established the foundational agreements, it is time to move on to **SMART goals**. A SMART goal is a mnemonic for a goal that is *Specific, Measurable, Achievable, Relevant, and Time-Bound*. These goals should be established first for the individual team members to deepen their skills and contributions to the team. Normally, these are established as part of the semi-annual or annual review cycle. As the leader of the team, you should have visibility into everyone's SMART goals so you can help guide them in the direction they intend to travel.

Finally, every Scrum Sprint and Release should have a SMART goal as well. This should be developed in partnership with the PO and the Development Team. A series of well-executed Sprint Goals will naturally lead to the attainment of the **Release Goal** for the product, since each Sprint is a stepping stone to the Release delivery.

We are working within the context of Scrum, so there is also an expectation that you, the leader, will ensure goals embrace **Agile principles** by being transparent, flexible, and adaptable. Improvements to the goals should be iterative, and the team must review and reassess their goals and strategies regularly.

At a minimum, the Sprint Goal should be reviewed at the end of the Sprint in the Sprint Review and during the Retrospective event. Team working agreements should be reviewed at the end of each calendar quarter to ensure they are still in alignment with the team's needs. Remember, every time you add or remove a team member, that is a trigger to review all the tools you are using to establish role clarity, expectations, and goals.

Summary

In this chapter, we have explored how to identify hard and soft skills for your distributed team. We studied things to look for to ensure a good fit into your team for the individuals you interview. Then, we discussed how proper onboarding can make your new team members effective contributors sooner and become fully engaged in your team and work.

Once your team is established, you need to build and maintain an inclusive team culture, so we looked at ways in which you can do that, both with and without the help of your HR department. Finally, we studied how setting expectations and goals will help individual team members to advance their skills and deliver on the product. When you implement these tools and techniques and apply the Agile principles to them, your team will become a healthy, collaborative engine for delivery.

In the next chapter, we are going to examine how you can leverage this foundation and cultivate a strong distributed team culture that can overcome any challenge it faces.

6

Cultivating a Strong Remote Culture

As we learned, remote work presents new challenges not faced by co-located teams. In traditional office environments, teams have spontaneous interactions and can readily see the non-verbal cues of their teammates. These things naturally foster communication and camaraderie. While difficult, cultivating a cohesive remote team culture is essential for boosting engagement, satisfaction, and productivity.

This chapter dives into the key aspects of building a robust remote team culture. It begins with promoting open communication, which is the foundation of every successful team. This includes practical facilitation tips to ensure inclusivity, so all voices are heard. From there, the chapter moves on to strategies for encouraging team bonding, detailing how you can plan virtual activities and informal interactions to break down barriers.

To ensure individual contributions do not go unnoticed, we examine how you can build recognition and celebration into your team activities. This chapter will help you build a framework for recognition programs that will motivate and encourage team members. Finally, this chapter acknowledges that not all will go smoothly, so you will learn skills and strategies for identifying, preventing, and resolving conflicts.

In this chapter, we are going to cover the following main topics:

- Promoting open communication
- Encouraging team bonding
- Recognizing and celebrating achievement
- Resolving conflict

Promoting open communication

This section addresses the importance of establishing open communication within your remote team. As a foundation, it is worth ensuring that we have a shared understanding of what is meant by "open communication." Open communication is the free, honest exchange of ideas and information without fear of ridicule or reprisals. This is the bedrock of trust for your team. High-level collaboration and problem-solving are not possible without this foundation of openness.

The role of communication in remote work

Communication is the root cause of all team success and failure. Everyone who has worked in business and on any type of team can provide examples of communication breakdowns that sink a project. Conversely, promoting communication with your team will have the opposite effect – you will more easily attain your goals.

For distributed teams, communication is more challenging. There are no spontaneous face-to-face interactions; you cannot bump into your teammates in the break room. Time zone challenges are also a barrier to successful communication; the need for asynchronous communication can delay responses and lead to misunderstandings.

All these challenges can be addressed with careful planning and forethought. Key elements to bear in mind are to ensure that all team members receive the same information at the same time. All team members should be included in decision-making processes and have opportunities to communicate their ideas and reservations openly. Remember, the ultimate reason behind these elements is to ensure a safe environment where everyone feels comfortable sharing ideas and feedback.

Applying techniques for open communication

Distributed teams are highly dependent upon technology to survive. As a distributed team leader, you need to set out early to create guardrails defining the best ways to use the diverse types of technology at your disposal. It is helpful for the team to collaborate with you on defining the general outlines of communication expectations. This will be examined in more detail in *Chapter 7* when working agreements are addressed.

In the interim, it is important to consider several factors when determining the best communication channel for the goal. For example, a team that is working with new technology may need to meet face to face frequently as they define their designs and best practices. A **synchronous communication channel**, such as Zoom or Webex, is the best option. If your team is not the group making this decision, make sure you have an avenue where you can ensure their feedback is considered.

Conversely, **asynchronous communication channels** such as Slack or MS Teams will be well suited for documentation review. Project management software such as Trello, Asana, or Jira is are wonderful asynchronous communication channels to keep everyone up to date on the progress of each person's work. The most important thing is to ensure everyone knows which channel to use for which situation.

As the team defines this, also be sure to consider urgency. For example, if the team was planning to use a certain tool to build part of the product, and it has been found to be ineffective, that is an urgent scenario you may need to address in your communication channel planning.

The tools cannot do all the work for the team either. There is an expectation that everyone on the team, not just you as the leader, has some *basic facilitation skills* to use. Anyone on the team can request a meeting for whatever purpose they have. Having the right to call meetings also demands the responsibility to accommodate various time zones and effectively facilitate the sessions.

At a minimum, every meeting must have some form of a lightweight *agenda, a defined purpose, and a goal* for the meeting. Whoever called the meeting must ensure that everyone who attends is contributing, even the quiet team members. Simple techniques such as "round-robin," where each person is called by name to get their ideas and input, are remarkably effective. Polling and voting are also helpful techniques if there are multiple options to be decided among. This focus on inclusiveness will make discussions more robust and decisions sound.

Finally, as the individual calling the meeting, a *post-meeting follow-up* should be sent to all attendees and interested parties. The follow-up needs to include any decisions that were made and the logic supporting them. If there are still unresolved issues, the follow-up needs to include a plan and schedule for addressing them and identifying the owner of the follow-up actions.

As you model these expectations, you will be demonstrating how to effectively communicate openly within the team. You will also set the foundation for the trust that is needed as you move forward in building a robust remote team culture. The next section examines how to encourage the next level of collaboration and camaraderie within the team.

Encouraging team bonding

The importance of team bonding, or cohesion, is hard to overstate. While many organizations have formal career path planning and formal employee retention strategies, they often overlook the value of investing in team cohesion. An old saying goes that people do not leave companies, they leave leaders. Here, we consider whether it is not just the leader but the whole team that can trigger employee departures.

Team cohesion can be garnered in simple, informal ways. For example, adding something lightweight to the normal Scrum events can create a bond within the team. I worked with a team once that used a deck of vocabulary flashcards at the start of each Daily Scrum event. The word from that day was then expected to be used every time the team members saw each other for the rest of the day.

This practice had dual benefits. First, on a very casual level, the team members were bonding over the creation of a shared new language. Additionally, they always had a way to break the ice with each other and begin even difficult topics with something light-hearted, humorous, and human.

Benefits of bonding

The benefits of team bonding are pervasive throughout the organization. The ripples will extend well beyond your team, and we need to examine a few of the key reasons behind these broad benefits:

- **Trust**: Proper team function relies upon the ability of individuals to trust each other. This is especially important for remote Scrum Teams where, each day, the individuals hold each other accountable for their work in the Daily Scrum. Knowing they can rely on each other to do what they committed to and will engage openly and honestly with their colleagues is the core of the trust the team needs to move to high performance.

- **Communication**: When team members trust each other and their leaders, they will more easily practice open and honest communication. Collaboration is increased with open communication. The net result of this is that you will see your team members engage in conversation, chats, and problem-solving spontaneously. You can expect to see better designs and reduced misunderstandings with fewer conflicts.

- **Productivity**: The end goal of every team, team leader, and product owner is high productivity. When your team is cohesive, you can expect to see the workload balanced. You will also see that when someone finishes their work early, they automatically volunteer to assist their team members with whatever tasks remain. Adding these up leads to increased productivity.

- **Creativity and learning**: One of the key elements for team bonding is the inclusivity you are establishing. Related to this is the ability and willingness of your team members to learn from each other. As the team members bond, they come to respect and admire the work of their peers. This combination of learning and new perspectives will generate greater creativity in your products and enhanced approaches to problem-solving.

- **Morale and motivation**: Successful teams balance fun and work; the adage "work hard, play hard" applies to most Scrum Teams, whether remote or co-located. Adding fun and opportunities to get to know each other will re-energize team members. They will be able to connect on a deeper level as they step away from work and into a more informal environment. These deeper connections are an excellent way to increase the likelihood of employee retention.

While this list of benefits is not all-inclusive, it certainly highlights the benefits you will gain from focusing on more than just the delivery of the product. As you focus on team bonding, the time you spend will result in benefits far beyond your team. This also has the potential to ripple throughout the organization.

Techniques for team bonding

There are many benefits to team bonding; now, we need to examine some ways in which you can create a cohesive team. Many of these approaches are simple and cost-effective; your biggest challenge will be in the scheduling.

Often, the team members in one part of the globe take the brunt of working odd hours to accommodate the other half of the planet. In this, like all other events you schedule, be sure to share that burden across all team members. In this way, you will ensure that no one region feels slighted. As a rule, you can rotate by Sprint or by Release. Note that rotating each Sprint can be challenging for the team to create healthy routines.

Some common techniques you can use include **icebreakers**. There are myriad options you can find online; one of my favorites is "Would you rather?". In this session, you present team members with two options; both are equally desirable or undesirable. Each person must make their selection aloud. This icebreaker helps people enjoy their tastes, similarities, and differences.

Another option to add to the repertoire is to find some interactive, **online games** you can play. There are virtual escape rooms and trivia games on a variety of topics that you can rotate through. One go-to that helps make the world seem to be a smaller place is www.virtualvacation.com. In this game, clues are provided, and your team attempts to guess the global location. You can select a country, region, or the entire world. As a bonus, this can also be used in conjunction with your efforts related to cultural inclusivity.

As you plan and execute your **team bonding program**, you will need to balance several things. First, there must be a balance between these gatherings and the team's workload. Additionally, work with team members to understand which days and times align best with everyone.

Next, balance the activities so some events appeal to the introverts on your team and others appeal to the extroverts. Finally, balance interest and engagement. Also, keep in mind that if you host these events too often, fewer people will attend, and those who do attend may not engage, or worse yet, multitask during the event. As with all things Agile and Scrum, host Retrospectives on these events at the end of each event. Something as simple as a Roman vote (thumbs up or thumbs down) can give you valuable feedback.

A final note on team bonding – there is a common technique you can introduce to your distributed team that will have multiple benefits. It is called a "personal user manual." This technique requires each team member to write down key elements that will help others work with them.

One team's user manual included topics such as these:

- My preferred communication channels are:
- I like to receive feedback in this manner:
- What energizes me at work is:
- One fun fact about me is:

When you provide your team with fun tools such as these, it enhances team cohesion, enables faster onboarding, and reduces the potential for conflict. It also gives you immediate insight into how to keep your team members engaged and focused.

Fostering informal connections

It is a wonderful idea to have a formal team bonding program. Equally important is to enable informal avenues for communication, sharing, and bonding. One way to do this is to establish a "virtual water cooler" channel in your Teams room or Slack team. This channel will be a replacement for bumping into your team members in the break room.

In this channel, you can seed conversations with open-ended topics. For example, you can ask @ everyone what their favorite fall sport or television program is. Another approach is to post your review of a movie you saw and ask for other thoughts. The more seeding you do, the more likely it is that the team will take over and add their own "conversations."

Another common tactic to add is to hold the occasional team lunch, coffee break, or happy hour. These are meant to be informal gatherings and give your team members much-needed face time separate from the important work they are doing. As in all things, be sure to balance these informal but scheduled events within the context of your larger bonding program to ensure you do not burn out the team. Balance is the key; with the right balance, the team will keep coming back for more.

Recognizing and celebrating achievements

For distributed teams, distance can result in feelings of isolation and working as an unnoticed cog in a larger system. Your efforts toward team building can help by creating a sense of belonging. While a sense of belonging will address the interpersonal aspects of the team, it does not address the need for professional recognition.

As the leader of a distributed team, you are responsible for ensuring achievements are recognized and celebrated. You will need to establish what behaviors will be recognized and establish a culture where recognition is not just top-down, but also peer-to-peer.

Developing a recognition program

Developing a program for recognition may sound daunting, but it can be lightweight and informal. All that is required is forethought regarding the type of behaviors and accomplishments that you want to reward.

The psychology of recognition is grounded in rewarding positive outcomes and reinforcing desired behaviors. Recognition programs improve engagement and retention when designed well. There are a few key objectives to keep in mind as you develop your team program:

- Make sure that rewards and recognition are *achievable* by everyone on the team. For example, if you only have one fully qualified user experience engineer, creating an award for "best user interface" is not a good idea. In effect, it will mean that, by default, there is only one person who could reasonably achieve that award, and so disincentivizes everyone else.

- Set *clear criteria* for recognition. For example, if you are working with a new Scrum Team, you may want to use your recognition program to reinforce Scrum Values that are new to the team.

- Ensure the recognition is *timely*. Once an achievement has occurred, recognize it as soon as possible after the event. Scrum itself provides a nice framework for this in the time-boxed sprint itself. Use the Sprints and Releases as milestones to guide your recognition.

- Be *specific and sincere* in your gratitude. Do not use the same thank you speech or email for every accomplishment you recognize.

- Enable *multiple channels* for recognition. There should be leader-driven rewards and peer-to-peer avenues for recognition. The peer-to-peer avenues should be simple and could even be a unique Teams or Slack channel where virtual high-fives are given. This can also reinforce your efforts towards team bonding by creating a team culture of gratitude and recognition.

As you embark on building your program, be sure to allow customizations so you can tailor the rewards to the individuals achieving them. For example, not everyone will want a large, public acknowledgment and would prefer to be recognized privately. Tailoring to the individual's desires also helps your team members feel seen as the unique contributors they are.

Celebrating success

Next is to work with your leaders and team members to establish what celebration of success needs to look like for the team within the context of the larger organization. It is common for team recognitions and celebrations to be informal and feed into the larger, formal celebrations at the department, division, or company level.

Formal programs at a larger scale usually consist of monthly, quarterly, or annual recognitions celebrated at all-hands events. Candidates for these awards are pulled from nominations throughout the organization. This is where your informal team awards can come into play by raising visibility for your team members.

From an informal perspective, celebrations can vary from verbal praise, an achievement dashboard, or small tokens that are sent to individuals to online cash reward cards or company gear. There are many ways to recognize the hard work of your team members. The important part is to make sure you establish something and stick with it.

Resolving conflict

Conflicts are inevitable. In a distributed Scrum Team, these conflicts can be exacerbated by physical distance, cultural differences, and a lack of real-time interaction. Successfully managing and resolving conflicts is critical to maintaining a productive and positive work environment.

It is important to note that not all conflict is bad. Constructive conflict can build a stronger team and a better product. Furthermore, keeping your team grounded in the Scrum Values of *commitment, courage, focus, openness*, and *respect* is helpful. Specifically, *openness* and *courage* demand that team members bravely and honestly share conflicting opinions in a respectful way. Scrum is designed to help teams leverage conflict to help them design better solutions.

Finally, understanding the most common types of conflict that arise on remote teams can help you be proactive and, hopefully, prevent some conflicts from occurring.

Common conflicts

Remote teams face a variety of unique challenges that can lead to conflict, including the following:

- **Miscommunication**: Digital communication lacks the non-verbal cues that you recognize in face-to-face interactions. Tone, intent, and urgency can be lost in written messages, leading to frustration or resentment. Misinterpreted emails or chat messages can quickly escalate into larger issues if not addressed early.

- **Cultural differences**: Remote teams often span multiple countries and time zones, bringing together a diverse range of cultural backgrounds. Differences in communication styles, work habits, and expectations can create misunderstandings. For example, in some cultures, direct feedback is considered rude, while in others, it is a sign of transparency and efficiency.

- **Lack of accountability**: In remote environments, it can be difficult to track individual contributions and hold people accountable for their work. Conflicts may arise when team members feel others are not pulling their weight or when expectations for deliverables are unclear. This can lead to resentment, blame, and a breakdown in trust.

Early identification and prevention

As a leader, a portion of your daily work is recognizing the early signs of conflict in your remote team. For example, you may observe that you are suddenly being included in IMs between two members regarding work details. This can be a passive-aggressive way for individuals to display their distrust of each other. As a leader, this is your cue to step in and investigate what is going on. Early identification can prevent issues from escalating and impacting team morale. Some common signs include the following:

- **Disengagement**: Team members who become less communicative or disengaged during meetings may be experiencing frustration or conflict with others

- **Passive-aggressive communication**: Hostility may appear in the form of passive-aggressive behavior, such as sarcastic comments or deliberately slow responses to messages

- **Exclusion from discussions**: In some cases, team members may intentionally or unintentionally exclude certain individuals from important conversations, leading to feelings of alienation or resentment

Conflict resolution skills and strategies

Resolving conflicts in a remote team requires a thoughtful approach. You will need to leverage both facilitation skills and structured conflict resolution policies to ensure issues are handled constructively and collaboratively. Additionally, these policies ensure that conflicts are addressed consistently and fairly.

Facilitation skills for conflict resolution

Effective conflict resolution starts with strong facilitation skills. Team leaders play a key role in guiding the resolution process by creating a safe environment for open dialogue:

- **Active listening techniques**: In a remote setting, active listening is even more critical. This involves fully focusing on the speaker, acknowledging their concerns, and repeating what was heard to ensure understanding. Active listening encourages all parties to feel heard and valued, which helps de-escalate tension. Techniques such as asking open-ended questions and summarizing key points can clarify issues and reduce misunderstandings.

- **Mediating discussions**: In more complex conflicts, a neutral third party may need to mediate. Remote mediators can create structured conversations through video calls, ensuring each side has a chance to present their views. The mediator should establish ground rules for respectful communication, ensuring that participants stay on topic and focused on finding solutions rather than assigning blame. If you are unsure how to find a mediator in your organization, reach out to your manager or your HR representative for guidance.

- **Encouraging constructive feedback**: Teaching team members to provide feedback in a constructive, non-judgmental manner can reduce the potential for conflict. Encourage the use of "I" statements (e.g., "I feel" or "I noticed") instead of accusatory language, which can put the other person on the defensive. No one will admit to enjoying role-playing exercises, but in the case of providing constructive feedback effectively, practice will help immensely. Again, if you are unsure how to facilitate such a session, reach out to your HR representative for help.

Developing conflict resolution policies

To ensure consistency and fairness in handling conflicts, it is important to have clear, well-communicated conflict resolution policies in place. These policies should be visible and proactive, and aim to prevent conflict when possible. They should also be reactive, providing structured pathways for resolution when issues arise.

The following list is a guide to ensure that your conflict resolution policies are robust enough to support your team:

- **Setting clear communication guidelines**: Establishing clear guidelines for communication from the outset can prevent many conflicts from occurring. These should include rules around response times, appropriate channels for different types of communication, and expectations for tone and professionalism. Documenting these guidelines in your team agreements ensures that everyone is on the same page about the basics of communication, such as when to use email versus instant messaging.

- **Conflict escalation processes**: Define clear steps for escalating conflicts. For example, minor disagreements can be handled directly between the parties involved, while more serious issues might require intervention by you, the team leader. You will also need to recognize when the team leader needs to escalate to a manager or HR representative. Having an established process in place ensures that conflicts are dealt with promptly and fairly, preventing them from festering and affecting team dynamics.

- **Training in conflict resolution skills**: Investing in conflict resolution training for team leaders and employees can equip them with the tools needed to manage disputes effectively. This can include training on active listening, negotiation techniques, and cultural sensitivity. Providing regular training helps to foster a team culture where conflicts are seen as opportunities for growth rather than obstacles.

- **Creating a feedback loop**: After a conflict has been resolved, it's important to evaluate the process and outcomes. Was the conflict handled efficiently and fairly? Did all parties feel heard and respected? A post-conflict feedback loop can provide valuable insights for improving future conflict resolution processes and help to ensure that similar issues do not arise again. Establish this feedback loop as part of the initial definition of your conflict resolution policies to ensure there is no bias. Additionally, consider whether someone outside the team should be responsible for gathering and sharing the feedback.

All of these elements are essential to ensuring there are safe pathways toward conflict resolution. They also ensure that no favoritism is shown. Finally, they help by establishing guidelines for everyone to follow, which saves time and minimizes team disruption.

Encouraging proactive conflict resolution

Encouraging team members to resolve small disagreements before they escalate into larger issues is key to maintaining a healthy remote team. As a leader, this is yet another behavior you will model for your team. You will also provide the framework they need to successfully navigate these issues. The framework you need includes the following:

- **Building a culture of openness and trust**: Remote teams that emphasize openness and trust are more likely to resolve conflicts constructively. When team members feel safe expressing their concerns, they are more likely to address issues early rather than letting them simmer.

- **Checking in regularly with team members**: Regular one-on-one meetings between you, the team leader, and individual team members can provide a space for discussing concerns before they escalate into full-blown conflicts. These check-ins should be informal, with an emphasis on open-ended questions such as "*How are things going with the team?*" or "*Is there anything you'd like to talk about?*".

- **Encouraging peer accountability**: Fostering a culture where team members hold each other accountable can prevent many conflicts from occurring. Encouraging team members to respectfully call out issues as they arise helps maintain transparency and prevents small issues from snowballing.

While conflict in remote teams can be challenging, the thoughtful and proactive approach laid out here provides all the tools that you need to successfully master remote conflict. Remember to focus on clear policies, strong facilitation skills, and early identification and resolution. By fostering open communication, encouraging team accountability, and providing structured pathways for conflict resolution, remote teams can navigate disputes in a way that strengthens team cohesion and trust.

Summary

In this chapter, the key aspects of building a robust remote team culture were examined in detail. The foundation we built upon was promoting open communication, which is the foundation of every successful team. This included practical facilitation tips to ensure inclusivity, so all voices are heard. From there, the chapter moved on to strategies for encouraging team bonding, detailing how you can plan virtual activities and informal interactions to break down barriers.

To ensure individual contributions do not go unnoticed, we examined how to build recognition and celebration into your team events. Finally, this chapter acknowledged that not all will go smoothly, so you will need skills and strategies for identifying, preventing, and resolving conflicts.

In the next chapter, we will examine how to use effective communication to establish teamwork agreements. These will help you and your team prevent conflict and increase productivity.

Effective Communication and Working Agreements

For today's proactive and interconnected teams, effective communication is more than just exchanging information – it is about understanding the emotions and intentions behind the information. Effective communication and well-structured team working agreements are fundamental to building collaborative and high-performing teams. They ensure that all team members are aligned with the team's objectives, understand their roles, and are committed to shared goals.

This chapter explores the critical components of effective communication within teams, emphasizing the importance of choosing the right communication channels, creating robust working agreements, developing feedback mechanisms, and fostering cultural sensitivity. By mastering skills such as communication planning, agreement drafting, and consensus building, teams can enhance collaboration, prevent misunderstandings, and drive continuous improvement.

In this chapter, we are going to cover the following main topics:

- Choosing communication channels wisely
- Creating effective working agreements
- Creating feedback cycles for continuous improvement
- Cultural sensitivity in communication

Choosing communication channels wisely

What you say matters. How you say it is equally, if not more, important. First, remember that communication flows in two directions. Next, recognize that the communication channel, or pathway to give and receive information, matters immensely to the recipient and drives how your message will be received.

The richness of your selected channel refers to how quickly and effectively you will receive feedback when delivering information. The richest form of communication is in-person, face-to-face communication, where both verbal and non-verbal communication is readily available, and which triggers a real-time response.

Before crafting your communication, consider the richness of the response you desire. Here is a table for your reference. Use this table as you begin to define your message.

Communication Type	Information Robustness
Face-to-face	High
Video conferencing	High
Telephone conversation	High
Email	Medium
Handheld devices (IM/Text)	Medium
Written letters and memos	Medium
Formal written documentation	Low
Spreadsheets	Low

Table 7.1: Communication depth

Low information robustness means that the communication is more likely to be misinterpreted or applied incorrectly. This type of communication is best used for things that require permanence, and we will explore that next.

Defining communication objectives

Before you contemplate the richness of communication you need, begin by defining what you hope to accomplish with your communication. Do you need to make a decision? Do you need to share information? Your purpose can be anything – the key is simply recognizing that the purpose of the communication plays a significant role in determining the level of communication richness you need.

Further, you will consider how quickly you must deliver your message and how permanent it needs to be. For example, if you need to document how a decision was made, you do not need rapid, or synchronous, communication. All you need is a permanent record of what decision was made and it can be accessed asynchronously, so written documentation may be the perfect channel.

To help you think through your options, here is a table for your consideration as you begin communication planning:

Communication Type	Richness	Speed	Permanency
Face-to-face	High	Synchronous	Low
Video Conferencing	High	Synchronous	Low, unless recorded
Telephone	Moderate	Synchronous	Low
Email	Low	Asynchronous	High
Instant Messaging (IM)	Low	Varies	High
Written documentation	Low	Asynchronous	High
Spreadsheets	Liow	Asynchronous	High

Table 7.2: Communication planning chart

The more sensitive the information is, the richer the channel needs to be. It is also important to realize that communications may need more than one channel to land as needed. An example of this is an annual or mid-year performance review.

You will need to deliver the contents of the review in the richest way possible, face-to-face or via videoconferencing. At the same time, you will need a permanent record of the review and your interaction with the individual. In this case, you will choose high-richness, synchronous communication with low permanency – video conferencing or face-to-face. You will also reinforce this channel with low-richness, asynchronous communication with high permanency – written documentation.

This is a single example of the myriad communications you will need to deliver as a team leader. Each type of communication will need careful consideration and planning, which we will address next.

Communication planning

As referenced earlier, you need to clearly understand the objectives, or *purpose*, of the communication you wish to deliver. Communication that is only meant to share information will have a different purpose than communication you want to trigger a response. It is straightforward to understand the purpose of your communication.

That, however, is simply the first step in communication planning. Next, you will need to identify your *audience*. Whether your audience is one person or many, you will select your communication channel based on whether the message is high priority or low and what level of permanence is needed. Additionally, carefully consider whether the audience is within the team or outside the team. For example, you will have a different communication plan for stakeholders and senior leaders.

Which brings us to *crafting the message* carefully. Communication that is frequent and informal, like that within the team, needs less planning. It does, however, demand the same level of attention to the details of richness, speed, and permanence. Crafting these messages also demands clarity and conciseness.

For stakeholders and senior leaders, your communication planning will be more robust and will address richness, speed, and permanence, among other things. The team members need a greater level of detail than these colleagues and partners. Hence, it is important that your communication be *complete, concise, and tailored* to the level of detail they need. You will specifically target their areas of greatest interest or concern.

Finally, consider the *timing* of your communication. For distributed teams, synchronous communication can be challenging. For stakeholders and other external partners, asynchronous communication is acceptable unless you are delivering significant good, or bad, news. Those communications are always high-stakes and demand the richness of face-to-face or videoconferencing.

For your individual team members, again, asynchronous communication can be acceptable if the stakes are low. As a leader, the onus is on you to accommodate the schedules of others when the stakes are high. Similarly, when the stakes are high and the whole team needs to come together, such as when an issue arises, rich channels, backed up with permanent documents, are your best option.

As you practice communication planning, you will get better at it. Work with your peer leaders to learn tips and tricks from them. Finally, make sure you speak with the recipients of your communications to understand what will best serve them and their needs. This conversation is a great way to introduce your audience members to the idea of establishing a foundation for working together. Specifically, you will begin your work together by establishing agreements on how best to interact with each other, including communication methods.

Creating effective working agreements

Also referred to as team agreements, working agreements are the guardrails the team places around themselves and their interactions with each other. Much like Scrum, which is the guardrail for how they complete their work, these are commitments the team makes to each other on how they will work with each other. Well-defined agreements will cover a broad range of topics, including logistics, such as processes and tools, and cultural, such as values, accountability, and resolving conflicts.

While Scrum guides how the team will handle their work on the product since the framework defines the events and timeboxes the team will use, the agreements are the wrapper around the whole team. Your agreements are your preventive medicine for things that could go wrong within the team. While these are important for co-located teams, they are essential for distributed teams.

The key components you will need to address in your agreements must cover the following items:

- **Roles and responsibilities**: Clearly, the Scrum roles will need to be defined, and their responsibilities established. In these agreements, you will want your team to go further by explicitly stating things such as how code reviews will occur and that everyone is responsible for testing.

  Another step that must be defined is how the team will handle accountability. For example, if a tester does not report bugs that are found, what will happen within the team to correct the mistake and ensure it does not happen again?

- **Communication norms**: Significant conflict can be avoided on the team by establishing response time expectations and defining communication channels for distinct types of communications. For example, if a bug is found, what is the best way to communicate it – email? Work management tool? IM? Further, ask and define how quickly it should be reported and what priority the fix has.

  Also in this arena is the topic of significant developments. For example, if you are using innovative technology and one of the team members discovers it will not work for your product as designed, how will this be escalated so that appropriate focus is given to the issue?

- **Decision-making processes**: Every team will need to make decisions, and starting your work with this process defined, as a team, will serve you well. In Scrum, decisions are driven by those doing the work – this means the team. Gaining complete consensus on every decision is unrealistic, so using a tool called **fist-to-five voting**, or something like it, can simplify your decision-making efforts.

  In fist-to-five voting, the goal is to establish a method by which individuals can have their concerns addressed while not preventing a decision from being made. From a process perspective, it works like this: An option, or decision, is laid out before the team that covers the who, what, why, how, and impact of the choice. The team then votes by using their fingers (in-person) or a number when remote. The options are as follows:

  - Zero/fist: No way, I strongly disagree with this

  - One/one finger: Hold on, I have concerns that need to be discussed

  - Two/two fingers: I could be convinced, but have reservations

  - Three/three fingers: I am okay with this option

  - Four/four fingers: I agree with this option

  - Five/five fingers: I completely agree

  This can be used in one of two ways. First, it can be used at the beginning of the discussion to draw out areas of concern for the presented option and then another decision-making tool, such as a majority vote, can be used after full discussion and, if needed, modifications to the option.

Second, it can be used both to start the discussion and to vote on the option. In this case, the team needs to agree that when the majority is at three or greater, then the decision can move forward. This is how the team can agree to disagree and move forward.

While the method of decision-making is up to the team, the essential element is to ensure there is an agreed-upon method.

- **Resolving conflict**: Despite all your work establishing working agreements, conflict will still arise, so the team must have a defined agreement for what to do when something comes up. At a minimum, the team should agree that, due to the lack of richness, email should not be used for conflict resolution.

  In some cases, conflicts between individuals can get hot, so agreeing to a "safe word" can be decided upon to prompt the next steps. This safe word then triggers a cooling-off period and an escalation of the conflict to someone else on the team for help in resolving it. Again, the specific steps and procedures are up to the team. The important part is to ensure the processes and escalation points are defined in advance.

Once your team has addressed and agreed upon your working agreements, it is time to *implement* them. The first step is to formalize them by *documenting* them and making them visible to all team members. An excellent location for this is the Teams' site or Slack channel. Everyone needs to have easy access to them so they can be followed and referenced.

Then the team needs to consider and decide upon a *cadence* for reviewing the agreements. When new members are added to the team, this should prompt a review of the agreements. When your team is stable, it is best to link your review cadence to the Scrum cadence. For example, linking agreement review with a quarterly release cadence can create an easy schedule to follow. As you work with your team, you will notice when a review is needed. You can address this in any Sprint Retrospective rather than as a separate topic during quarterly planning. The important thing is to review them when the team changes or if you notice agreements are not being followed as they were intended.

Finally, team working agreements are pointless if the team does not *enforce* them. This can be done professionally and respectfully. There is an adage that says, "praise in public, correct in private," and it is appropriate to consider here. When someone violates an agreement, the person who spots it should address it with the individual one-on-one. Then, it should be shared with the whole team, and the agreement should be re-committed to by the group.

If this sounds like a topic for a working agreement, it is. This falls under the key element of resolving conflict, covered earlier. Once you have established working agreements and the review cycle, the team is off and running. The review cycle for your agreements is an entry point for a larger discussion about continuous improvement, which is covered in our next section.

Ensuring continuous improvement with feedback cycles

One reason for the success of Scrum is its principles of inspecting and adapting based on experience and the latest information. This is effective for creating a high-quality product. When applied to your team, it helps drive a culture of high performance, transparency, and trust.

Feedback can be assumed to have negative connotations. For the sake of clarity, in our context, *feedback is the giving and receiving of both positive and negative information*. Feedback is a tool to highlight areas of excellence and identify areas for improvement. When designing your feedback program for your distributed team, it is important to keep this in mind and use it to set the stage for the team.

The first step in building your feedback cycles is to *nurture a growth mindset*. In many ways, you are already doing this with your focus on creating a cohesive team that establishes foundational trust. A growth mindset, however, goes beyond this and demands that everyone sees mistakes as lessons, as opportunities for growth.

You begin to establish this mindset as the leader by openly sharing your current and past professional mistakes and subsequent lessons. When you demonstrate that failure is not fatal, rather it is enlightening, you will create a safe space for your team members to do the same.

Next, you will need to work with the team to *build a feedback framework*. A simple framework to use is your recurring one-on-one meetings with your team members. This enables you to provide positive and constructive feedback and to receive the same. It becomes more complicated when you consider how individuals give feedback to each other, where those formal meetings don't already exist.

In this case, you may create a Teams channel for positive callouts, enabling team members to give each other shout-outs in real time. Further, when the feedback is constructive, it is a good idea to establish feedback ground rules in your working agreements. For example, the team may create an agreement that says positive feedback can be given publicly or privately, verbally or in writing, while constructive feedback must be delivered privately via videoconferencing.

The next critical step is to *provide training* to team members, so they know how to give and receive feedback. Your HR representative may have material already built for you to utilize, so be sure to engage with them for support. At a minimum, individuals need to learn the basics of feedback. These steps are essential, though how they are delivered is unique to each individual and situation:

1. **Affirm the recipient's identity**: Demonstrate that you understand their situation and the feedback is not a character attack.

2. **Provide context**: Define the time and place in which the mistake or inappropriate behavior took place.

3. **Describe the mistake**: State what you saw without jumping to conclusions as to why the behavior happened.

4. **Explain the impact**: Share how the behavior or mistake affected you, the team, the customer, or the product.

5. **Provide suggestions**: Offer your ideas on ways to handle similar situations in the future; ideally, collaborate in the moment with the recipient to find solutions that feel comfortable for them.

There are many tools to provide feedback, but they all should have these five elements within them. Using these steps ensures that individuals will feel seen and valued while also having a sense of accountability.

With individual feedback loops created, it is also important to note that, despite training, not everyone will feel comfortable giving you, the leader, feedback directly. Since that is the reality of feedback, you also need to implement feedback frameworks to enable *anonymous feedback*.

You can use surveys sent out on a regular basis to gain deeper insight into how the team is feeling overall about your leadership, the product, and the Scrum implementation. Also, you can request that a neutral third party hosts a Retrospective specific to these topics. In either case, be *transparent with the team* about the feedback received and share your plans for addressing it.

As you establish the normalcy of feedback, positive and negative, you will set the stage for continuous improvement. The insights individuals gain from the feedback and the changes they make as a result will create a growth mindset for the team. This mindset ensures that everyone will hold themselves and others accountable for their outcomes while also ensuring that every situation is viewed as an opportunity for growth. This is what continuous improvement is all about.

Cultural sensitivity in communication

Working with a distributed, multicultural team increases the likelihood of making cultural mistakes in your communication. Cultural sensitivity is more than understanding diverse holidays celebrated globally and withholding judgment on those traditions; it also includes understanding and adapting to them in your communications.

The first step is to begin a journey toward *understanding cultural dynamics* on the team, meaning you need to understand cultural traditions and communication styles, and identify areas where conflict may easily arise.

To identify cultural biases within the team, you should look for cultural norms and values across multiple areas. The best starting point for this is to start with yourself and your cultural biases – *self-awareness* and your personal cultural defaults.

Identifying, sharing, and being transparent about your own cultural biases will help build trust within the team. For example, I am from the Central region of the United States. My cultural defaults include being very direct and dominating conversations. As you reflect on your biases, consider how they will affect your team members from other cultures and share the results of your reflections.

The next step is to *identify the cultural differences across the team* and begin to understand the cultural norms and values of those nations or regions. There are myriad resources online for you to do research and certainly reach out to your HR representative, also. However, the best source for this information is your team members themselves. Culture is painted in broad brush strokes, while your communication style will need to be tailored to the specific persons within their cultural context.

Context is critical. Context is a specific aspect of communication styles. Some cultures are high-context and others are low-context. **High context cultures** include body language, tone, and overall context in their communication style. **Low context cultures**, however, base their communication style on explicit, straightforward communication; precision in communication is valued. This contextual difference can create issues rapidly if not handled with care. This blog post from www.countrynavigator.com describes the contextual differences and impact perfectly:

> *"People and teams working in low context cultures take the words spoken literally and prefer having comprehensive information to prepare for a meeting or task. In this sense, there is an expectation for precise agendas, information packages, and meeting reports. On the other hand, high context cultures do not prefer formalized information and would find the previous approach too technical or unnecessary. They prefer face-to-face meetings over documents, as they find relationship-building and close contact necessary for establishing mutual understanding."*

As you navigate the cultural differences on your team, engage with your team members so they share their cultural defaults and establish their *preferences in communication*. You can document these preferences on the team site or, better yet, encourage each person on the team to create their own "home page" on your team site. Here, they can share their cultural experiences and default behaviors in a candid and light-hearted manner.

Non-verbal communication

Non-verbal communication is crucial, especially in distributed work environments, where all face-to-face communication is onscreen. Nonverbal communication is the process of conveying information without using spoken or written words. It includes visual cues such as facial expressions or body movements; auditory cues such as tone of voice, pitch, and pace of speech; and time usage. These nonverbal cues are combined with spoken or written words to provide a fuller picture of the message being sent.

As in all things related to communication, *self-awareness* is the best starting point. You must understand that your own non-verbal cues can help you understand those of others. Become conscious of how you sit or stand when delivering good news; understand how these forms help convey the intent of your message. Try the same for delivering unwelcome news or raising an issue on your product. Use the self-view of your videoconferencing tool to help you see yourself as others see you in your communication delivery.

Active listening is a wonderful way to ensure you are receiving messages as they are intended. This means that you are fully focused on what is being said. This is a full-body level of engagement where you are leaning in slightly, maintaining eye contact, and giving affirming nods that you are present. You are not multitasking or allowing your mind to wander; you are fully engrossed in what is being said and grasping the meaning as well as the intent.

Active listening is an effective way to build rapport with your team members. Another technique to help you is known as mirroring. *Mirroring* involves subtly matching the other person's body language. Not only will it help you build rapport, but it can also help with your active listening. Finally, it can help develop empathy by helping you understand the emotions behind the message being delivered.

One final note on non-verbal communication is regarding *gestures*. Hand gestures exist across cultures, but the meanings of these gestures can be quite different from one location to another. Cultural sensitivity includes understanding common gestures and their meanings for your team members.

An example of this cultural context is what my culture considers the peace sign. To me, lifting the index and middle finger and then separating them to create a "V" shape means "peace." In some countries, this symbol means victory, and in yet other countries its meaning can be offensive. This is why it is important to understand your own frequently used gestures and what they could mean to your colleagues. Additionally, encourage everyone on the team to do the same.

As author Matthew Syed said, "*Diversity science...will prove to be a key source of innovation.*" Adding cultural sensitivity and inclusion into your communication can only help your team move toward high performance and establish the excellent communication your product demands.

Summary

This chapter has underscored the importance of communication in fostering a cohesive and high-performing team environment. By carefully selecting communication channels, teams can ensure that their messages are delivered clearly and efficiently, reducing misunderstandings, and enhancing collaboration. Strategic communication planning – defining clear objectives, understanding the audience, and crafting concise messages – serves as the bedrock for effective interaction.

Creating effective working agreements through collaborative drafting and consensus-building empowers team members by clarifying roles, responsibilities, and communication norms. This process not only establishes expectations but also fosters a sense of shared ownership and commitment to the team's goals. Regularly reviewing and updating these agreements keeps them relevant and responsive to the team's evolving needs, ensuring sustained alignment and accountability.

The implementation of feedback loops and a culture of continuous improvement is crucial for ongoing team development. Structured feedback mechanisms encourage open communication, allowing team members to share insights and address challenges proactively. By analyzing feedback and being accountable for improvement, teams can enhance their performance and adapt to changing circumstances.

Cultural sensitivity in communication emerges as a vital component in your distributed and global teams. Understanding cultural dynamics, adapting communication styles, and promoting inclusivity enable teams to navigate cultural differences effectively. By valuing diverse perspectives and addressing cultural misunderstandings, teams can turn diversity into a strength that enriches collaboration and innovation.

Integrating these principles equips teams with the tools to navigate the complexities of modern collaboration. As we shall see in our next chapter, these are also the foundations for clear accountability, motivation, and performance.

8

Managing Performance and Motivation

Managing performance and motivation within a distributed workforce requires a different approach than traditional, in-office settings. Leaders must develop skills in performance analysis, virtual assessment, and motivational strategies to ensure their teams remain engaged, productive, and aligned with organizational goals. This chapter investigates the complexities of managing performance and motivation for remote workers, offering insights into setting clear performance metrics, conducting meaningful reviews, and creating effective career development pathways in a virtual environment.

Performance management in a remote setting is not just about tracking progress; it involves a deep understanding of how to set measurable goals that align with both individual and company objectives. This requires leaders to adapt their strategies to the needs of a distributed team, using data-driven techniques to identify strengths and areas for improvement. Motivation also plays a crucial role in ensuring that remote employees stay engaged and committed. The absence of face-to-face interaction can make it challenging to maintain motivation, but with the right tools, leaders can create a culture of trust, recognition, and accountability.

In this chapter, we are going to cover the following main topics:

- Setting and monitoring performance metrics
- Motivation techniques for remote workers
- Conducting remote performance reviews
- Career development for distributed team members

Setting and monitoring performance metrics

Effective performance management begins with establishing clear, measurable goals that guide employees' efforts and align with the organization's objectives. In a remote work environment, where face-to-face interactions and spontaneous check-ins are limited, setting and monitoring performance metrics become even more critical. These metrics serve as the foundation for evaluating productivity, identifying growth opportunities, and ensuring that all team members are contributing meaningfully to both the product and the company's success.

The challenge of managing a distributed team lies not just in defining what success looks like but also in accurately tracking and assessing progress in real time. Leaders must develop a deep understanding of performance metrics that are **Specific, Measurable, Achievable, Relevant, and Time-Bound (SMART)**, tailoring these indicators to fit the unique dynamics of remote work. This section explores how to set up effective performance goals, choose the right tools for tracking progress, and analyze performance data to gain actionable insights.

In this section, we will break down the steps to establish robust performance metrics, discuss the best tools for tracking remote productivity, and offer strategies to interpret data effectively. Understanding these elements is crucial for any leader aiming to build a high-performing, cohesive remote team that is aligned with both short-term milestones and long-term business goals.

Understanding performance metrics

Key Performance Indicators (KPIs) are success indicators that show how well individuals and teams are doing compared to goals or planned accomplishments. Using metrics effectively not only helps the team leader understand how the team and individuals are doing but also provides leading indicators for the leader to see when things are amiss.

It is critical for all Scrum Teams to measure their progress, understand what the metrics mean, and act when there are unwelcome deviations. Here are the top 10 KPIs for you to use with your distributed team. In combination with understanding the metric, you also need to know how it can signal trouble, so details for this are also included:

- **Sprint burndown chart**:

  - **What it is**: A graphical representation of the amount of work remaining versus time during the Sprint.

  - **How it works**: The y axis represents the amount of work (measured in story points, hours, or tasks), and the x axis represents the time remaining in the Sprint. The ideal burndown is a steady decline toward 0 as the team completes work.

Identifying trouble:

- **Flatline at the beginning**: If the line remains flat early in the Sprint, it suggests that the team may be slow to start or that there are obstacles delaying work

- **Sharp decline at the end**: A significant drop toward the end of the Sprint may indicate that the team is rushing to complete tasks or has over-committed

- **Burndown line not reaching 0**: If the work remaining doesn't approach 0 by the end of the Sprint, it could mean that the team overestimated their capacity, mismanaged priorities, or encountered unforeseen issues

- **Sprint velocity**:

  - **What it is**: Measures the amount of work (story points or tasks) completed during the Sprint compared to previous Sprints.

  - **How it works**: The team's velocity is calculated as the total number of story points or tasks completed in a Sprint. Velocity trends can help with forecasting and Sprint Planning.

  Identifying trouble:

  - **Declining velocity**: If velocity drops across multiple Sprints, it may indicate reduced team capacity, inefficient processes, distractions, or unplanned issues (such as defects or production support).

  - **Significant fluctuations**: Erratic velocity, where one Sprint is much higher or lower than the next, may indicate that the team struggles with estimation or has inconsistent work practices. While some fluctuations are normal for teams, large variations are unusual and deserve further investigation to determine whether they are due to typical complexities or other forces acting on the team.

- **Sprint Review feedback**:

  - **What it is**: Feedback from stakeholders and **Product Owners** (**POs**) during the Sprint Review/demo, where the team showcases completed work.

  - **How it works**: The Sprint Review allows stakeholders to assess whether the delivered work meets expectations and provides value.

  Identifying trouble:

  - **Frequent changes requested**: If stakeholders frequently request changes during the Sprint Review, it could indicate misalignment between the PO and the team, poor initial requirements, or a misunderstanding of the business needs

  - **Low engagement or dissatisfaction**: Lack of enthusiasm or negative feedback from stakeholders may signal that the delivered work is not meeting the intended objectives or delivering enough value

- **Sprint Retrospective**:

  - **What it is**: A team meeting held at the end of a Sprint to reflect on what went well, what didn't, and what can be improved

  - **How it works**: The Retrospective encourages team members to discuss successes, challenges, and areas for improvement in a safe, collaborative environment

  Identifying trouble:

  - **Recurrent issues**: If the same problems are identified in multiple Retrospectives without resolution, it may indicate a deeper, systemic issue with process, communication, or team dynamics

  - **Lack of engagement**: If team members are disengaged or reluctant to provide input, it could suggest low morale, a fear of voicing concerns, or burnout

- **Sprint Goal achievement**:

  - **What it is**: The extent to which the Sprint goals (defined at the beginning) are met by the end of the Sprint.

  - **How it works**: At the start of the Sprint, the team commits to delivering specific outcomes (user stories and features). Achievement is measured by whether those outcomes are delivered as promised.

  Identifying trouble:

  - **Inability to meet goals**: Frequently missing Sprint goals can indicate over-commitment, poor estimation, unplanned work (e.g., bug fixes), or scope creep

  - **Constantly changing Sprint goals**: If Sprint goals frequently change mid-Sprint, it could indicate poor backlog management, unclear priorities, or external disruptions

- **Work in Progress (WIP) limit monitoring**:

  - **What it is**: A technique to limit the number of work items that are actively being worked on at any time.

  - **How it works**: Teams monitor the WIP limits to ensure that no more than a set number of work items are in progress. Exceeding WIP limits often leads to inefficiencies and context switching.

  Identifying trouble:

  - **Exceeding WIP limits**: If WIP limits are consistently exceeded, it may indicate over-commitment, poor task prioritization, or team members taking on too much work at once

  - **Work bottlenecks**: If a specific phase (e.g., development or QA) has many items stuck in progress, it signals a bottleneck that needs to be addressed

- **Cumulative Flow Diagram (CFD):**

  - **What it is:** A visual representation of the work in various stages of completion over time, tracking the flow of tasks through the system (e.g., backlog, in progress, and completed).

  - **How it works:** The CFD shows how tasks are distributed across stages and how work is progressing. It helps to spot bottlenecks and monitor the flow of tasks.

  Identifying trouble:

  - **Widening areas:** A growing gap between tasks "in progress" and tasks "done" could indicate a bottleneck. For example, a widening in the "development" area suggests too much work is stuck in that phase.

  - **Stagnation in early stages:** If tasks are not moving from the "to-do" or "in progress" columns, it may signal blockers, miscommunication, or dependency issues.

- **Defect rate during Sprint:**

  - **What it is:** Measures the number of defects found during the Sprint, typically in new code or features

  - **How it works:** The defect rate is tracked to identify the quality of the work being delivered within the Sprint

  Identifying trouble:

  - **High defect rate:** If many defects are found during or after development, it indicates quality issues, possibly due to rushed work, poor testing, or unclear requirements

  - **Defects spilling over into future sprints:** If defects are consistently carried over into the next sprint, it suggests that quality control and testing processes are inadequate

- **Team engagement and focus factor:**

  - **What it is:** Measures how much time team members spend on sprint-related tasks versus distractions, such as meetings, support tasks, or non-sprint activities.

  - **How it works:** A focus factor is calculated as the percentage of total time spent on actual sprint work. A low focus factor indicates too many distractions from the sprint work.

  Identifying trouble:

  - **Low focus factor:** If the team is consistently distracted by non-sprint tasks, it indicates that Sprint Planning may be ineffective, or that the team is being pulled in too many directions

  - **High task switching:** Too many ongoing tasks or distractions from outside the sprint can indicate that the team is not fully dedicated to sprint priorities

- **Impediment tracking:**

  - **What it is**: A log of blockers, challenges, or impediments that prevent the team from making progress during the Sprint

  - **How it works**: Agile teams track impediments and raise them in daily stand-ups or through tools such as issue trackers

  Identifying trouble:

  - **Recurring impediments**: If the same impediments are raised repeatedly across multiple Sprints, it suggests that fundamental issues are not being addressed

  - **Long time to resolve impediments**: Delays in resolving impediments suggest a lack of support, unclear ownership, or insufficient resources

By using these Sprint execution measurement methods, Agile teams can not only measure their progress and performance but also identify areas of trouble early on. Spotting trends such as declining velocity, unaddressed impediments, or bottlenecks in the flow of work helps teams adapt quickly and continuously improve their process.

Establishing performance goals

Scrum inherently helps align the work of the team with the *organizational goals*. Each product in the organization is aligned and funded within the umbrella of strategic planning. Each PO presents and aligns their *product roadmap* to the executive steering committee for funding and approval.

As part of this process, the PO will have gained insight into why the product and the features they are working on are important. They need to continually share this information with the team, so team members understand how their individual contributions help attain the corporate goals.

From a tactical perspective, walking the team through the corporate goals, then to the product alignment, is the first step. Once product alignment is established and understood, it is time to share and closely examine the product roadmap. The roadmap lays out what features will be delivered when to achieve the corporate goals.

It is important to note that the roadmap, as presented by the PO, is an estimate of what will be done, in what order, and at what time. This roadmap is presented to executive leaders for approval, but it is only a planned approach. The next level of planning, the *release plan*, is where detailed, *collaborative planning* occurs.

Collaborative planning is essential to obtaining team understanding and buy-in. For your KPIs to resonate with your team, they must have a *sense of ownership* over the goals and believe they are realistic and obtainable. Once the release plan is collaboratively established (see *Section 4*) you will derive your goals from it because you know what will need to be accomplished and by what time to deliver the product as approved by executive leadership.

Monitoring performance metrics is also guided by the Scrum framework. The twelfth Manifesto principle, in fact, encourages regular reflection. This encompasses the individual as well as the team. Each Sprint timebox is an opportunity to set a **Sprint Goal** that is aligned with your **product release plan**. Each Sprint Goal is a stepping stone on the path toward release and roadmap completion. In fact, each Scrum timebox, from Sprint through release, is a goal-setting opportunity.

Finally, make sure you help your team members understand how their work, as individuals, contributes to the Sprint, release, roadmap, and corporate goals. Explicitly defining this connection helps you set performance goals for each person as well. For example, if you have a development team member whose primary skill is development, it is straightforward to make that connection.

Following the same example, if that developer-skilled team member does not contribute to helping other developers or pitching in with testing others' code, you need to also paint the picture of how that resistance is slowing down the team's goal attainment.

As you can see, what is happening is two-fold. First, you are helping team members to see how their task-level activities support the corporate strategic objectives. Second, you are helping them see how the **Scrum Values** also help attain those goals more effectively by demanding that everyone help in every way possible to attain the Sprint Goal. This is the Scrum Value of *commitment*.

Finally, you are committing to following up on those goals. Goals are only valuable as long as they are being monitored, assessed, and adjusted as the situation changes. This commitment is demonstrated by conducting regular performance reviews.

Motivation techniques for remote workers

Remote work is redefining the traditional workplace and introducing new psychological dynamics that affect team member motivation. Remote workers, even when hybrid-remote, face challenges such as social isolation, lack of direct supervision, and difficulty separating professional from personal life. These elements can affect their motivation, engagement, and overall morale.

One of the key elements of Agile and Scrum is the need for team members to feel that they are an essential part of a larger whole; a sense of belonging is necessary for this to happen. The sense of *isolation and loneliness* common among remote workers is a clear impediment to this foundational element of a team.

The best approach to combat this is to have regular face-to-face conversations with your team members. That applies to you as the leader and to the peer team members. Your regular one-to-one meetings are a great foundation, and insisting that Scrum events occur on camera whenever possible will also help.

Closely related to the sense of isolation is the blurring of the *boundaries between work and home*. Though team members may feel isolated, they may be unable to separate from their work sufficiently, leading to overworking and burnout. As a leader of the team, you will need to pay attention to the timestamps on messages and emails from your team members. These can provide clues for you to investigate.

When you recognize a pattern of long working hours for any one of your team members, you will need to address it immediately and on camera. You need to probe to determine whether the timestamps represent continuous working hours or whether there is a situation where this team member is working split hours.

If a team member is working long, continuous hours, you will need to step in as leader and coach them to help them find acceptable boundaries and determine whether they are being unduly influenced to commit time at this level. When external influence is at play, you should step in to protect your team members. When you take steps like this, you will be demonstrating that the team member is a valued member of the team who is seen as an essential contributor to team success.

Factors influencing motivation

Let us begin by defining the two types of motivation. The first type of motivation is **intrinsic motivation**. This type of motivation is driven by internal rewards, such as personal growth, interest in what you are doing, and the satisfaction of overcoming challenges you face in your work. When you are working on something personally or professionally and you lose track of time, you are intrinsically motivated.

The other type of motivation is **extrinsic motivation**. Rewards such as salary increases, bonuses, and promotions are examples of external motivation. Public recognition is also an external motivator and can be used in virtual meetings to help motivate your team members.

Daniel Pink demonstrates in his ground-breaking book, *Drive: The Surprising Truth About What Motivates Us*, that people are far more motivated by intrinsic motivation than by extrinsic rewards. Specifically, the studies he references indicate that people are motivated specifically by autonomy, mastery, and purpose. Let's investigate this in more detail.

Autonomy means that we are empowering our team members with the freedom to make decisions about their own work. This finding aligns perfectly with the Agile Manifesto, where we are driving our decisions to the individuals closest to completing the work. Being repetitive about the team's self-organization and the individual's empowerment to make decisions will reinforce the intrinsic motivation of your team.

Next, consider *mastery* and what that means in the context of your distributed Scrum Team. This intrinsic motivator is all about our need, as people, to get better at what we do each day. This links directly to the Manifesto principle of applying technical excellence – this is something we must strive toward and may never fully attain.

Finally, Pink's work indicates the final intrinsic motivation for people is purpose. Our *purpose* is the alignment of our work to something that really matters. In Scrum, our work is aligned with a specific product that is, in turn, aligned with the overall strategic objectives. Clearly defining the corporate mission to serve with the product your team members work on will align their need with the purpose of the work they are doing, thus enhancing their intrinsic motivation.

Implementing motivational strategies

Both intrinsic and extrinsic motivation types are needed for every team. While Daniel Pink's research suggests that intrinsic motivation is more important, it is essential to remember that both are necessary. Considering this, let us think about simple ways to appeal to both sides of the motivation coin:

- **Aligning work with professional goals**: As team leader, working closely with your team members to understand their career goals and ambitions is necessary. With this information, you can better tailor the team goals toward meeting their long-term objectives.

- **Implementing rewards systems**: An excellent strategy here is to develop a structured recognition program within the team that offers both intrinsic rewards, such as attending a training class, and extrinsic rewards, such as public recognition or bonuses. When implementing such systems, take care to maintain quantitative measures and minimize any appearance of favoritism.

- **Providing regular feedback and coaching**: Regular, constructive feedback helps team members see the impact of their work, enhancing intrinsic motivation, while also guiding them toward extrinsic goals such as recognition. Spending time with your team members to make sure they understand where they fit and how they contribute and reinforcing their role in the success of the larger organization will pay dividends in motivation, high performance, and team cohesiveness.

- **Remaining informed and flexible**: Studies into the psychology of the remote worker's motivation are gaining ground, and much more will be revealed in the coming months and years, so remain up to date with the latest trends and research in this area. Closely related to this is being willing to experiment with innovative approaches and discontinuing ones that the team has outgrown. Today's recipe for motivation and fulfillment will not necessarily be tomorrow's ideal approach. Again, this links back to the Agile value of experimentation and failing fast to attain the best results for your team.

For team leaders, understanding individual and team motivation is the best path forward in creating your high-performing, distributed Scrum Team. These strategies and practical steps address the psychological factors affecting your team and resolve the challenges you will face in distributed team leadership. The focus, as always with Scrum, is on creating a supporting and engaging virtual environment that fosters individual motivation and intricately links it to organizational strategy.

Conducting remote performance reviews

Preparation is the cornerstone of effective performance reviews. This is true whether in person or remote, although extra preparation is required for remote interviews. The objective of the performance review is to reinforce constructive feedback you have already been delivering while enabling the team member to feel valued and heard. Finally, it is also the objective to ensure that clear goals and expectations are set for your team members.

Preparing for remote performance reviews

The very first step in preparation for the performance review is *gathering data*. In this process, you will seek comprehensive information about everyone's performance. You will be seeking quantitative metrics such as task completion rates and deadlines met, as well as qualitative metrics. Your qualitative metrics will include peer and customer feedback.

Next is *creating an agenda* for the review. Here, you will outline the topics to be discussed. Key points will include achievements, areas for improvement, career goals, and actionable next steps. Send the agenda in advance to ensure the team member has adequate time to prepare. If you already have your data gathered when you send the agenda, you can include this information as well.

Another key step to remember is ensuring *technical readiness*. Make sure to test your video conferencing tools in advance and verify that you have a stable internet connection. Provide your team members with clear instructions on how to join your meeting and what to do in case there are unforeseen technical issues.

Establishing privacy and confidentiality will help put your team members at ease. Select a private, quiet location to conduct their review. Tell them where you will be located and provide guidance on what type of location they should choose as well. For example, neither party should be in a public space such as a coffee shop or restaurant. Then, assure them that their feedback and concerns are valuable and will be handled with discretion.

Finally, *set a positive tone* as the performance review begins. Begin and end the conversation with an acknowledgment of the team member's contributions. Follow your agenda and remain focused on growth and development rather than criticism. Since you have been providing feedback to your team members regularly, there should be no surprises for you or them during the formal review process.

When you regularly invest in providing feedback to your team members, the additional steps for preparing for the formal review are lightweight and should be no real burden. Your team members will appreciate the time you have taken to give them a safe space in which to receive feedback and partner with you on their professional growth and development.

Performance reviews have limited impact when they are conducted without understanding and compassion for the team member's short-term and long-term goals. This means the onus is on you to understand what the team needs now, and how the team's needs can align, in the long term, with the individual's goals.

Career development for distributed team members

Career development is an essential component of employee engagement and retention. It can be particularly challenging in remote work environments. Providing clear career pathways and opportunities for growth not only motivates team members but also ensures that your organization has a skilled, adaptable workforce.

Remote career development requires deliberate strategies to address unique challenges, such as limited face-to-face interactions and the absence of traditional mentorship opportunities.

The value of career development

Career development, as a formal method of staff development, has become a focal point for many companies. There are both tangible and intangible benefits to taking a systemic approach with your remote team members. The most easily recognizable benefits are greater employee satisfaction and longer employee retention.

Employees who see a career path for themselves in your organization are more likely to remain engaged and loyal to the company. Beyond visualizing themselves in your organization over the long term, encouraging skill enhancement benefits both sides of the relationship. For the team member, they are gaining marketable skills, and for the team, they are aligning themselves to the organizational needs. This creates an avenue for innovation and efficiency that may otherwise be unavailable.

Finally, how team members feel matters greatly. When they see a leader taking an interest in their career aspirations, they will feel seen, valued, and necessary to the success of the team and the whole organization. As a result, they become your organizational ambassadors.

Overcoming challenges in remote career development

There are challenges with career development, whether the team is collocated or remote. The greater challenge, however, remains with the remote team. For collocated individuals, it is easier, and more convenient, to include them in meetings, brainstorming sessions, or even coffee breaks to advance their careers. For your remote team members, you will need to be calculating about providing them with the boost they need to move toward their career goals.

- **Visibility**:

  Remote employees may feel their contributions are overlooked compared to in-office peers

  Transparent recognition and feedback systems help bridge this gap

- **Communication barriers**:

  Without regular in-person interactions, employees may find it harder to express career aspirations

  Structured career conversations ensure employees feel heard

- **Access to resources**:

  Limited access to training programs or mentors can hinder growth

  Virtual learning platforms and online mentorship programs are crucial solutions

Skill development and training opportunities

Assisting team members with their career aspirations requires more than conversation and regular review; it takes tactical action. You, as the leader, need to identify key skills for your team and align those skills with the future needs of the team and the individual. Start by identifying the team's immediate needs.

- **Technical skills**:

  - Proficiency in digital tools and platforms used in remote work (e.g., project management software and communication tools)

  - Industry-specific skills that contribute to job effectiveness

- **Soft skills**:

  - Communication, collaboration, and emotional intelligence are critical for remote team success

  - Self-management skills, including time management and adaptability, are essential

- **Leadership skills**:

  - Remote team leaders require unique capabilities, such as virtual team building and conflict resolution.

Training is an excellent starting point for helping your team members. The next step is to provide them with tactical support:

- **Guidance and support**:

  - Mentors provide career advice, share experiences, and guide employees in navigating organizational challenges

  - Remote mentorship ensures that employees feel connected and supported despite physical distance

- **Skill transfer**:

  - Mentors help mentees acquire specific technical or interpersonal skills needed for growth

Virtual mentorship can be a challenge, so work with your HR department to determine whether a program already exists. A key thing to consider when working with your HR department is the framework in which they monitor mentoring programs.

- **Matching mentors and mentees**:

  - Use structured programs to pair mentors with mentees based on career goals and interests

  - Leverage technology to facilitate the matching process and ensure compatibility

- **Scheduling regular check-ins**:

  - Establish a consistent cadence for mentorship meetings to maintain momentum

  - Use video calls to foster a personal connection and enable deeper discussions

- **Goal-oriented mentorship**:

  - Define clear objectives for the mentorship relationship, such as skill-building, role preparation, or career planning

  - Track progress and be willing to adjust goals as needed

Recognition and celebrating success

Just as you work hard toward your career goals, so do your team members. Since that is the reality for everyone, it is essential that we provide recognition for their efforts and accomplishments:

- **Celebrating achievements**:

  - Recognize accomplishments through virtual ceremonies, newsletters, or team meetings

  - Highlight employee achievements on internal communication platforms

- **Peer recognition**:

  - Encourage team members to recognize each other's contributions using platforms such as Bonusly or Slack integrations. If none of those platforms are in place, you can use a Slack channel or a Teams chat dedicated to recognition.

- **Performance-based rewards**:

  - Tie recognition programs to tangible rewards, such as bonuses, promotions, or additional responsibilities

Skill development and training

Some elements of career development are made difficult by distance. For example, remote team members may feel overlooked when some staff are remote and some are on-site. Taking care to ensure recognition systems are transparent and impartial can help alleviate this perception. Additionally, ensuring that you are having regular face-to-face conversations with your team members will help them feel seen and valued.

As part of these ongoing conversations, desired skills for the team and the organization should be laid out before team members. This may open doors for their career path that they had not considered.

For example, there are well-defined career paths in technical disciplines. These are beneficial for the advancement of the product and the whole organization. However, they should not be the only opportunities made available to your team members. There are also soft skills, such as those we covered in our *Chapter 5: Recruiting and Forming a Distributed Scrum Team* on hiring, that will be mutually beneficial.

You must differentiate for your team members which trainings are related to career development and which are obligatory. You may require all team members to take training and attain a certain proficiency level with tools the organization and teams use every day, such as conferencing or code management tools.

Some soft skills may also be required training, such as conflict resolution and communication training. Some key trainings that are beneficial for all team members are self-management skills, communication skills, and emotional intelligence training.

Finally, if a team member has the desire to move into leadership as part of their career path, this could be an avenue for non-required training. In this area, you can encourage training in team building and conflict resolution. Make sure that you are partnering with your HR partners to make sure your guidance is in alignment with the organization's overall career development objectives.

Establishing virtual mentorship programs

One of the traditional methods for career development has been mentorship programs. For distributed teams, this can prove particularly challenging, but this is still a vital tool for you to use. First, let us affirm the value of a mentor.

Mentors provide career advice, share experiences, and offer valuable connections within the organization. The advice a mentor provides can help the team member become more certain about their chosen career path. By sharing experiences, the mentor ensures the mentee does not repeat well-worn mistakes.

Finally, do not overlook the value of intra-organizational connections. As mentors share connections with your team members, your team is creating a network of support throughout the organization. This provides your whole team with a backup system to help them overcome obstacles.

If a mentorship program does not yet exist in your organization, work with your HR partners to establish one. A mentoring program should be structured such that mentors are paired, based on their expertise and interests, with mentees who share similar interests and goals aligned to their expertise.

Artificial intelligence is an excellent tool to use to establish a pairing program for mentors and mentees. You can also set it up to go further to ensure that the pair are also compatible in temperament. These individuals may come to the matching process with separate goals, but after being matched, they need to create shared goals that are timeboxed and tracked.

Finally, a word on recognition. When you establish training, career development, and mentorship programs, it is crucial that you build in celebrations of success. These efforts can range from the simple, such as a newsletter, to the extravagant, such as a graduation ceremony, or anything in between. The important point is that when your team members follow up on their training and career pathing goals, they are recognized and celebrated.

Summary

Performance management in a remote setting is not just about tracking progress; it involves a deep understanding of how to set measurable goals that align with both individual and company objectives. This requires leaders to adapt their strategies to the needs of a distributed team. In this chapter, we have explored how you can set and monitor goals to help your team members meet their product and Sprint Goals. We also explored techniques you can use to motivate your team members.

Finally, we created actionable steps for you to use when holding distributed team performance reviews and the elements needed for career path development. When you put these actions into practice, you will create an environment of skill development, mentorship, recognition, and career advancement, ensuring distributed employees feel valued, supported, and empowered to achieve their professional goals. By implementing these strategies, organizations can build a motivated, loyal, and high-performing remote workforce.

In the next chapter, we will address the ways in which collaboration tools and software can help your team members in their training, mentoring, and collaboration efforts. These tools will keep them engaged, driving them toward their career goals, and help build a high-quality product.

Part 3: Technology for Distributed Team Success

Technology has a pivotal role in helping distributed Scrum Teams succeed and enabling close collaboration. We will examine a selection of collaboration tools, software for work tracking, and platforms that support remote pair programming and code reviews. We will also explore implementing Continuous Integration/Continuous Deployment (CI/CD) techniques on distributed teams.

This part has the following chapters:

- *Chapter 9, Collaboration Tools and Software*
- *Chapter 10, Remote Pair Programming and Code Reviews*
- *Chapter 11, Continuous Integration and Continuous Deployment (CI/CD)*
- *Chapter 12, Security and Compliance in Remote Work*

9

Collaboration Tools
and Software

Distributed Scrum Teams are becoming common as organizations embrace remote work and global talent pools. These teams, often spread across different time zones and geographic locations, leverage the principles of Scrum to manage their workflows effectively. However, the distributed nature of these teams introduces unique challenges that traditional co-located teams do not face.

In this chapter, we explore how collaboration tools and software can address these challenges, ensuring that distributed Scrum Teams operate as effectively as their co-located counterparts. Collaboration tools bridge gaps by providing platforms for real-time communication, task tracking, and collaborative work on documents and code repositories.

In this chapter, we're going to cover the following main topics:

- Work management tools
- Communication platforms
- Collaborative document and code sharing
- Choosing secure and reliable tools

Work management tools

Work management tools are essential for distributed Scrum Teams to organize, prioritize, and track their efforts. These tools provide a centralized platform for managing the complexities of technical initiatives and Agile processes, ensuring transparency, accountability, and alignment among team members. For distributed teams, they bridge the gap created by distance and time zones, offering real-time visibility into project progress and fostering collaboration across the globe.

Here are the key benefits of work management tools:

- **Enhanced transparency**: All team members can view task progress, blockers, and deadlines

- **Streamlined Agile processes**: Tools align with Scrum practices such as Sprint Planning, Backlog management, and Retrospectives

- **Improved accountability**: Teams can assign ownership of tasks and monitor responsibilities

This section explores essential features, examples, and best practices for using work management tools and maximizing their capabilities.

There are key features to seek in your selected work management platform. Gaps in any of these areas can impede the success of your distributed Scrum Teams. Let us examine the essential features you will need.

Task and project tracking

At the very least, your work management tool needs to track user stories and the tasks needed to complete them. Different organizations have implemented different portfolio levels, such as Initiatives and Epics, so you must consider these elements too. From the team operating procedures, you will need the following items:

- The ability to create and assign tasks, set deadlines, and monitor progress in real time

- Hierarchical organization, including epics, stories, and subtasks, to align with Scrum processes

- Visual tracking methods, such as Kanban boards and Gantt charts, provide at-a-glance updates

Sprint and backlog management

While the Product Owner and Scrum Master are tracking the progression of work at the story and task level, they have additional responsibilities. The Product Owner will need specific functionality to organize and prioritize their backlog and refine the user stories. As you search for a tool, seek one that meets these needs:

- Tools to manage product backlogs, prioritize items, and allocate tasks during Sprint Planning

- Sprint-specific dashboards to track the velocity and capacity of the team

- Burndown and burnup charts for monitoring Sprint progress against goals

Reporting and analytics

Scrum is a data-driven process framework. Every day, the team examines its Sprint burndown chart and uses this information to identify areas of trouble. Whichever work management tool you select, you will have some essential reporting needs. You will need to survey your distributed teams to ensure their needs are understood and considered. Minimally, you will need a tool that has the following:

- Automated generation of reports on team performance, task completion rates, and blockers
- Metrics for Agile **key performance indicators** (**KPIs**), such as velocity, cycle time, and lead time

Integration capabilities

No work management tool stands alone; it exists in an ecosystem of tools. Since this is always the case, be sure to take needed integrations into account as you seek your work management tools. You will be looking for the following:

- Seamless integration with communication tools, version control systems, and document-sharing platforms
- APIs and third-party apps to extend functionality and streamline workflow

Now that we have looked at essential features, examples, and best practices in detail, let us explore a few work management tools.

Examples of popular work management tools

A simple internet search will reveal many options for your work management platform. In this section, I provide a list of some of the most commonly used Agile work platforms. In the preceding section, we offered a set of minimum requirements, and all platforms listed here will meet those needs. Additionally, we will see some highlights of the strengths of each platform for you to consider.

Jira: Jira is a robust project management tool developed by Atlassian, primarily used by software teams to track tasks and issues:

- Tailored for Agile teams, with robust Sprint management features
- Customizable workflows, filters, and dashboards for detailed tracking
- Integration with development tools such as Bitbucket and CI/CD pipelines

Trello: Trello is a visually oriented, card-based project management tool that helps teams organize tasks and workflows:

- Simple, intuitive Kanban boards for task visualization

- Ideal for smaller teams or less complex projects

- Power-ups to add advanced functionalities such as calendars and integrations

Asana: Asana is a versatile work management platform designed to help teams plan, track, and manage tasks effectively:

- Focus on task dependencies and team collaboration

- Features such as project timelines, workload balancing, and milestone tracking

- User-friendly interface for non-technical team members

Monday.com: Monday.com is a customizable project management solution known for its visually appealing boards and easy-to-use interface:

- Highly customizable task and project tracking

- Automation capabilities for repetitive tasks

- Collaborative features such as shared boards and team notifications

Here, we have highlighted specific elements for each platform. If you prefer a specific platform, but an element here is not listed as one of its strengths, research the platform more deeply. It is likely that it does offer that feature, but this list is not exhaustive.

Exploring best practices for work management tools

There are many *best practices* that will be specific to the work management platform you choose. However, there are some things that are true regardless of platform. The old saying "garbage in, garbage out" comes to mind. As you introduce your work management platform, remember that Agile practices should drive your tools and not the other way around.

Your teams need to come to a consensus on the best Agile practices in your organization. Once this is settled, you can replicate it within the workflow. The risk of starting with the offered workflow within the tool is a mismatch with what will work best in your organization.

Further, as Agile and Scrum expand in your environment, the consistency of your implementation will simplify roll-up reporting across products, divisions, and strategic initiatives. This consistency will also simplify budgeting and strategic alignment of work. Agile teams, within reason, can tweak their processes to streamline them and make them more efficient. The baseline best practices for work management across an organization are as follows:

Establishing consistent workflows:

- Define clear task statuses (e.g., To Do, In Progress, Done)

- Standardize naming conventions for tasks, epics, and subtasks

Optimizing tool usage for agile practices:

- Align tools with Scrum ceremonies, such as Sprint Planning and Retrospectives

- Use task priorities and deadlines to drive focus and ensure timely delivery

Encouraging team engagement:

- Regularly update tasks to ensure accuracy and prevent bottlenecks

- Promote team ownership by involving members in customizing workflows

Leveraging automation:

- Automate routine tasks such as notifications, status updates, and reporting

- Use integrations to reduce manual data entry across platforms

Work management tools are indispensable for distributed Scrum Teams, enabling them to navigate the complexities of remote collaboration. By providing structure, visibility, and alignment, these tools help teams stay focused on delivering value. However, the effectiveness of these tools depends on proper implementation, team buy-in, and alignment with Agile and Scrum principles. When used strategically, work management tools empower distributed teams to overcome the challenges of distance.

While these tools are powerful aids to your distributed team, they cannot replace effective communication and collaboration amongst team members. Selecting and using the right communication platforms can aid your teams in ways that work management tools alone cannot.

Mastering communication platforms

Effective communication is the backbone of any successful Scrum Team, and its importance multiplies in distributed Scrum. In such environments, the absence of face-to-face interaction necessitates tools that facilitate both synchronous and asynchronous communication. Communication tools help bridge geographical and temporal divides, ensuring that team members remain connected, aligned, and collaborative.

For distributed Scrum Teams, these platforms are essential for the following:

- **Daily Scrum**: Quick, focused check-ins to align team efforts
- **Scrum events**: Planning, Reviews, and Retrospectives that keep the Scrum cycle on track
- **Daily collaboration**: Sharing updates, clarifications, and decisions promptly

In this section, we explore the types of communication tools and their roles in the Scrum framework.

Types of communication tools

There are two types of communication platforms we will explore. They are synchronous and asynchronous; each is vital to the success of your distributed teams. *Synchronous communication* platforms represent real-time, in-the-moment communications, and they take multiple forms. It is likely that you will need all these forms to be successful. Let's explore a few of them:

- **Instant messaging platforms**: Tools such as **Slack** and **Microsoft Teams** offer *channels and threads* to facilitate rapid group discussion. They also include *direct messaging* to facilitate, or replicate, walking over to someone's desk for a quick chat. Another key feature of these platforms is the ability to search message history and receive real-time notifications.

- **Video conferencing platforms**: **Zoom**, **Google Meet**, and **Microsoft Teams** provide virtual meeting spaces for distributed teams. Features such as screen sharing, breakout rooms, and recording capabilities enhance the effectiveness of team discussions and collaborative sessions.

- **Virtual whiteboarding platforms**: Some of the best examples of these tools are **Miro** and **Mural**. Both support visual collaboration for brainstorming, problem-solving, planning, and Sprint Retrospectives. Additionally, these bridge the space between synchronous and asynchronous communication since they can be used in both real time and across time.

The other side of this coin is *asynchronous communication*, which is a type of communication separated by time. Again, you will likely need all forms of these tools to be successful. Here is a snapshot of these tools:

- **Email and documentation platforms**: Traditional tools such as **Gmail** and **Outlook** are useful for formal communication and asynchronous updates.

- **Video and voice messaging tools**: Tools such as **Loom** and **Voxer** allow team members to record messages with context, saving time and avoiding scheduling conflicts. These can be particularly useful to enhance your distributed Scrum meetings when your disparate team members can record their video Scrum updates.

- **Work management features**: Built-in commenting tools in platforms such as **Jira**, **Asana**, and **Google Workspace** support asynchronous discussions directly within tasks or documents.

The role of communication tools

Communication platforms and effectively using them can differentiate between success and failure for distributed teams. The chief mechanism for keeping your Scrum framework going is the use of these tools.

You will use them to *facilitate Scrum events*. Zoom's scheduled calls and Slack's huddle feature enable short, focused updates. Video conferencing, screen sharing, and whiteboards allow teams to collaborate on Sprint Goals, discuss backlogs, and reflect on completed work.

One of the most dominant challenges facing all distributed Scrum Teams is *collaborative problem-solving*. Effective use of both synchronous and asynchronous communication platforms can resolve these challenges. Instant messaging helps teams resolve blockers without waiting for a formal meeting. Tools such as Loom allow members in different time zones to provide context or updates without needing live interaction.

Finally, and certainly not least important, is the role these platforms can play in *enhancing team bonding*. You can establish social channels and call them *#watercooler* or *#coffeebreak*. You can even go further by encouraging team members with similar interests, such as gaming or pets, to start chat channels on those topics.

Communication tools are the lifeline of distributed Scrum Teams, providing the channels needed to align, collaborate, and innovate. By leveraging a mix of synchronous tools for real-time interaction and asynchronous tools for flexibility, teams can ensure that distance and time zones do not hinder their productivity. The choice of tools should align with the team's needs, ensuring seamless integration into the Scrum framework. When paired with clear communication norms and practices, these platforms empower teams to operate cohesively, regardless of location.

Collaborative documentation and code sharing

Distributed Scrum Teams rely heavily on the ability to co-create, share, and manage documents and code in real time. These tools enable team members to work together seamlessly, regardless of location or time zone. For Scrum Teams, this is critical during activities such as writing user stories, creating technical documentation, managing product roadmaps, and developing and maintaining code bases.

Collaborative document- and code-sharing tools provide the following:

- **Real-time collaboration**: Multiple team members can work on the same document or code base simultaneously

- **Version control**: Track changes, revert to previous versions, and maintain clarity on contributions

- **Centralized access**: A single source of truth for documents, code, and related resources

This section examines the tools available for collaborative document and code sharing, their features, and best practices for effective usage.

Document collaboration

Agile and Scrum value working software over comprehensive documentation. That does *not* mean that documentation is unnecessary. In fact, lightweight, collaboratively developed documentation helps to keep team members aligned so they can create working software.

Google Workspace (Docs, Sheets, Slides) offers real-time co-authoring, comment threads, and version history. This platform also allows easy sharing and access control. Another excellent option is **Microsoft Office 365 (Word, Excel, PowerPoint)**, which provides powerful editing tools with cloud-based real-time collaboration. Additionally, there is tight integration in Microsoft to integrate its tools with enterprise ecosystems to ensure all platforms work together seamlessly.

Distributed teams also face unique challenges in onboarding new team members. Often, a new team member and their onboarding guide are not in the same time zone. This is where *knowledge management systems* can help. Examples include **Confluence** and **Notion**.

Confluence is ideal for storing and managing project documentation, meeting notes, and Retrospectives. It also integrates with Jira for linking documents to tasks and Sprints. Another option is Notion, which is a flexible tool for organizing project roadmaps, team wikis, and collaborative planning; it also combines notetaking, task tracking, and document creation in a single platform. As you select your platform for collaboration document management, make sure to include training and defining best practices as part of the implementation.

Collaborative code management

The challenges of physical distance can take their toll on code quality. Collaborative code management is crucial for distributed Scrum Teams because it simplifies these challenges by providing real-team visibility into code changes, facilitating communication, maintaining code quality, and ensuring everyone is working on the same version of the product.

Minimum requirements for code management include the following features:

- **Version control systems**:

  - **GitHub** is a widely used example of a platform specifically designed for code hosting, version control, and collaboration.

  - **GitLab** offers integrated **Continuous Integration/Continuous Delivery (CI/CD)** pipelines for automating builds, tests, and deployments.

- **Code collaboration features**:

  - **Branch management** allows developers to work independently on features, fixes, and experiments without affecting the main code base. This feature also supports *merging strategies* that align with Scrum release plans.

  - **Code review** support exists within good code management tools as well. They enable peer reviews with inline comments, and discussions can be triggered with pull requests.

  - **Pair programming** is often used by Scrum Teams. Pioneered in **eXtreme Programming (XP)**, this technique allows developers to collaborate on code. **Visual Studio Live Share** and **Code Together** are examples of tools that simulate the experience of pair programming. These are also excellent tools for debugging, mentoring, and solving complex problems.

Best practices for leveraging your communications platform

As you use document- and code-sharing platforms, there are best practices to keep in mind. First, *centralize documentation*. Your team must follow the precept of having a single source of truth for all project-related materials. It will also help improve usability when you *encourage consistent formatting*. Using templates for documents such as user stories, Sprint plans, and technical documentation can help you implement this strategy.

Code collaboration also has a set of best practices to follow. Start by establishing clear branching strategies to manage parallel workstreams. Leverage CI/CD tools to automate testing and deployment. This will increase team speed and maintain high quality in your product releases. Finally, if you aren't already doing so, expect code reviews. This will foster a culture of continuous improvement, ensure code quality, and share knowledge.

Collaborative document- and code-sharing tools are indispensable for distributed Scrum Teams, enabling seamless co-creation, streamlined feedback, and consistency. Document tools such as **Google Docs** and **Confluence** help teams stay aligned on plans and progress, while code-sharing platforms such as GitHub and GitLab ensure efficient, high-quality development processes. By implementing best practices such as centralized documentation, standardized workflows, and robust version control, teams can enhance collaboration, reduce miscommunication, and maintain a high standard of productivity and quality.

Choosing secure and reliable tools

Selecting the right tools for a distributed Scrum Team involves more than just functionality and user experience – it requires a focus on security and reliability. With sensitive data, proprietary code, and team communications often stored and exchanged on these platforms, ensuring data integrity and minimizing downtime are critical. A secure and reliable tool protects against data breaches, unauthorized access, and workflow interruptions.

For distributed Scrum Teams, the key considerations when choosing tools include the following:

- **Security**: Protecting sensitive project information, intellectual property, and personal data
- **Reliability**: Ensuring uptime, scalability, and seamless performance under various conditions

This section explores the aspects of security and reliability that teams should evaluate when choosing tools and provides actionable strategies for making informed decisions.

Evaluating security

Essential requirements for every platform you choose include core security features. Every platform should offer *data encryption*. Evaluate whether the platform offers encryption at rest and while data is in transit. Ideally, it would offer both, especially for platforms focused on messaging.

Next, ensure that *access control* is in place. Most platforms offer the ideal, which is **role-based access control** (**RBAC**) based on the role and function of the individual. In our current environment, which is rife with hacking, seeking a platform that offers **multi-factor authentication** (**MFA**) is an almost required enhancement.

Ensure you understand how the platform's parent organization handles *incident response* and *security updates*. The tools you are using should have real-time monitoring of suspicious activities and the ability to alert administrators using the platform. Look for consistent security patching and updates to address emerging threats.

Evaluating reliability

These platforms will be the lifeblood of your distributed team's productivity. Choosing excellent tools is irrelevant if those tools are unreliable. As part of your assessment of the performance of the tools you are considering, be sure to evaluate their **service level agreements** (**SLAs**). You will be seeking a high uptime guarantee of 99.9%.

Related to this is the need to understand the platform's *history of downtime*. Do research on past incidents that the platform experienced. Seek out the reasons why and look at the platform's user groups to understand how well the organization managed the downtime. Additionally, user groups can be a great investigation tool.

User groups are an excellent place to research the tool's past incidents to evaluate reliability.

User groups can also indicate the tool's *performance under load*, specifically whether the tool can handle large teams, high volumes of data, or complex tasks without significant slowdowns. They will also shine a light on *support availability* and the tool's *knowledge base*. A large and active user community can be a good indicator of reliability and a valuable resource for troubleshooting.

Best practices for choosing secure and reliable tools

It is probable that you have a robust information technology department, which has strong practices related to platform assessment and evaluation. As a member of or partner to that department, educate yourself on the best practices around tool assessment and selection.

You will need to understand how best to Conduct Comprehensive Evaluations using a tool evaluation checklist that covers functionality, security, reliability, and user experience. Request free trials or demos to test tools in real-world scenarios.

If possible, *involve the* team in decision-making . Engage team members to ensure the tool meets practical needs and aligns with existing workflows. Gather feedback from team members to understand their concerns and preferences.

Choosing secure and reliable tools is a critical decision for distributed Scrum Teams, as these tools form the foundation of collaboration, communication, and productivity. By evaluating a tool's security features – such as encryption, access control, and compliance – and its reliability in terms of uptime, scalability, and support, teams can make informed decisions that minimize risks and maximize efficiency. When paired with best practices such as team involvement, secure and reliable tools empower Scrum Teams to focus on their goals without worrying about technical disruptions.

Summary

Distributed Scrum Teams rely on collaboration tools to bridge the gaps caused by physical separation, time zones, and cultural differences. These tools play a pivotal role in ensuring that teams can communicate effectively, manage their work efficiently, and collaborate seamlessly on documents and code bases.

Work management tools provide the backbone for organizing Scrum workflows, enabling teams to track tasks, manage Sprints, and monitor progress with real-time visibility. Communication platforms further enhance collaboration by facilitating both synchronous and asynchronous interactions, ensuring that no team member is left out of critical conversations or updates.

Collaborative document and code-sharing tools enable teams to co-create and manage their work efficiently. From creating and managing documentation to collaborating on code with robust version control systems, these tools ensure that teams have a shared source of truth and a streamlined workflow. Implementing best practices such as centralized documentation, branching strategies, and regular code reviews fosters quality and consistency across the team.

Finally, selecting secure and reliable tools is paramount to ensuring the safety of sensitive data and the continuity of operations. By evaluating security features, reliability, and adaptability, teams can choose tools that align with their needs while mitigating risks.

Ultimately, the success of a distributed Scrum Team depends on choosing the right tools, implementing them thoughtfully, and continuously adapting them to the team's evolving needs. These are the foundational elements that must be in place to maximize the benefits of remote pair programming and code reviews, which will be examined in detail in the next chapter.

10

Remote Pair Programming and Code Reviews

When pair programming was made popular by **eXtreme Programming** (**XP**) in the early stages of Agile software development, teams were collocated. Remote teams were exceedingly rare at the time, so the initial set of best practices for this technique was focused on collocated pairs of programmers.

Remote work has transformed software development, necessitating effective collaboration in distributed environments. Remote pair programming and code reviews have emerged as critical practices to maintain code quality, enhance team productivity, and foster learning.

This chapter explores how to adapt traditional collaborative coding techniques to virtual settings, emphasizing the tools, skills, and best practices necessary for success. The discussion focuses on navigating communication challenges, building a culture of collaboration, and honing critical analysis skills to conduct meaningful code reviews. In this chapter, we're going to cover the following main topics:

- Best practices for remote pair programming
- Tools and technology for remote pairing
- Conducting effective remote code reviews

By the end of this chapter, you will be equipped with actionable strategies to thrive in remote software development and apply best practices for pair programming and code reviewing.

Best practices for remote pair programming

Pair programming is a technique where two programmers share a single workstation and work on the same piece of code at the same time. It is an important technique for all teams because it fosters knowledge sharing and improves code quality by allowing real-time feedback on the code being written. Since there is a real-time review of the code being written, the likelihood of bugs in the completed code is significantly reduced. An additional benefit is the enhanced communication between team members and the in-depth knowledge transfer taking place.

Collaborative coding techniques

There are two common models for pair programming. Regardless of which you choose, the roles for each model are the same. There is always a **Driver** and there is always a **Navigator**, but the role each plays is slightly different depending on the model. No person is always the driver or always the navigator; it's important to switch roles.

Now, let us examine the models more closely.

Driver-navigator model

- **Role definition**: The driver actively writes the code, while the navigator reviews the code in real time, offering suggestions and focusing on the bigger picture.

- **Maintaining balance**: Avoid overstepping roles; both participants should switch roles frequently to ensure engagement and equal contribution.

- **Effective communication**: The navigator should articulate thoughts clearly and provide constructive guidance without dominating the session.

Ping-pong programming

- **Alternating roles**: One developer writes a failing test (navigator), and the other writes code to pass the test (driver). Roles switch after every cycle. This is a combination of pair programming and **Test-Driven-Development (TDD)**.

- **Enhancing collaboration**: This technique promotes joint responsibility for testing and coding, ensuring both participants understand all aspects of the task.

- **Building momentum**: Regular switches keep the session dynamic and engaging, reducing the risk of fatigue.

Pair programming sessions should include time for discussing potential solutions and choosing the best approach. Before launching pair programming, make sure you have established methods to resolve differences of opinion, such as deferring to documented coding standards or temporarily implementing both solutions for later evaluation. Finally, ensure there is a continuous feedback loop in place. Encourage both developers to *offer and accept feedback openly* to refine solutions during the session.

Additional best practices include making sure that pair programming sessions are *planned*. You will need to define clear goals and the scope of the session before starting, so that you reduce the amount of time spent on unrelated items. These scheduled sessions also need to be *time-boxed* into manageable blocks with regular breaks to maintain focus and productivity.

After each pair programming session, the developers need to spend a few minutes discussing what went well and what could be improved. This brief *session Retrospective* will provide actionable insights to this pair of programmers and other pairs on your team. Pair programming has robust technical benefits and also improves team dynamics.

Tools and technology for remote pairing

Effective remote pair programming relies on using the right tools and technologies to overcome the inherent challenges of distributed environments. The tools chosen must facilitate smooth, real-time collaboration while minimizing technical barriers such as latency, communication issues, and workflow disruptions. There are some essential tools that make remote pair programming effective, including real-time coding platforms, video communication tools, and automation technologies. Further, there are best practices for optimizing technical setups to ensure seamless coding sessions, helping teams stay productive and engaged regardless of location.

As you expect, your developers will need *reliable video and screen-sharing* tools. Tools such as **Microsoft Teams**, **Google Meet**, and **Zoom** allow these capabilities. These tools enable scheduling as well, thus enabling *clear communication* while navigating code together. As you select your tools, keep in mind that you need to minimize latency and prevent unnecessary outages. Whenever possible, ensure that an *online whiteboard* is also available to help with code design questions.

An **Integrated Development Environment**, or **IDE**, is a software application that enhances the efficiency of code development. In the context of pair programming, many of these platforms, such as **Visual Studio Code** or **IntelliJ IDEA**, offer plugins such as **Live Share** or **Code With Me,** which, respectively, allow your team members to collaborate on the same code base in real time. Here, you will see shared debugging, synchronized cursors, and integrated version control. Additionally, these tools use intelligent conflict resolution mechanisms to ensure changes appear consistently on both ends, without delays.

Automating and integrating

Finally, encourage your team members to use automation and integration. Use your CI/CD pipelines to test and deploy quickly during pair programming sessions. This will ensure immediate validation of the code and that changes are committed, reviewed, and merged in real time. Finally, it is best practice to turn on logging for your pair programming sessions. Logging can help track decisions and ensure knowledge transfer for future sessions.

When you use the right tools and best practices for pair programming and include proper training, it becomes easy to implement in your team. Developers will create stronger relationships with their colleagues and the quality of your team's code, and the product will improve with additional eyes designing the solution. To better understand the tangible benefits of pair programming, let's explore real-world case studies that highlight its impact on productivity, code quality, and team dynamics.

Pair programming case study

Pair programming has been widely adopted by development teams to improve code quality, enhance collaboration, and accelerate problem-solving. By working in pairs, developers can catch errors early, share knowledge more effectively, and produce more maintainable code. While the benefits of pair programming are well-documented in theory, real-world case studies provide valuable insights into how teams successfully implement this practice and the measurable improvements it brings. The following case studies showcase how different organizations have leveraged pair programming to enhance productivity, strengthen team cohesion, and deliver higher-quality software.

Tribal Scale at McCain

Tribal Scale, a global innovation firm, partners with their clients to introduce and leverage best practices in their Agile, digital environments. During a collaboration with McCain, a leading food manufacturing company, the development team initially followed a conventional approach that excluded pair programming and TDD. This led to two significant challenges: a lack of context and knowledge transfer among developers, as individual team members worked in silos, and an absence of systematic testing, which resulted in gaps in business logic coverage. Recognizing these inefficiencies, the team adopted **extreme programming** (**XP**) practices, particularly pair programming and TDD. The transformation was remarkable – enhancing code quality, improving knowledge sharing, and even enabling the project to be delivered two weeks ahead of schedule.

The shift to pair programming introduced several key benefits, including more thorough collaborative planning, immediate feedback through real-time testing, improved documentation, and a seamless knowledge transfer process. While challenges such as resource intensity and compatibility between paired developers arose, these were managed through open communication, regular pair rotations, and structured feedback mechanisms. Ultimately, the experience demonstrated that while pair programming requires an upfront investment in time and resources, its long-term impact on efficiency, code maintainability, and team collaboration makes it a valuable practice for high-performing development teams

Conducting effective remote code reviews

Utilizing pair programming techniques does not eliminate the need for traditional code review. Code reviews are essential for maintaining code quality, fostering knowledge transfer, and ensuring adherence to coding standards. In remote environments, conducting effective code reviews requires structured processes, strong communication skills, and the right tools to overcome physical separation.

There are key skills and practices necessary for critical code analysis, identifying issues, evaluating code quality, and providing constructive feedback. You must also streamline review processes, such as establishing clear standards and leveraging technology to enhance collaboration. When analyzing code, the first step is to *identify issues*.

Only critical analysis can help you do that. The very first step is to understand the context in which the code was written. Developers presenting their code need to present the problem and the user story the code is meant to solve. Only with this information can the reviewers examine both the code and its alignment to the broader needs of the customers.

Train your team members to detect common **code smells**. This term is a way of expressing common anti-patterns that often exist in code. For example, using overly complex methods, duplicated code, or poor naming conventions are common code smells to watch out for. Another one is detecting functions that exceed a set line threshold may clue you into a need to refactor the code.

An innovative code review process is known as a **test-driven review**. A test-driven code review uses test cases, especially edge cases, to expose potential bugs in the code that may not appear until the code is live in a production environment. These are very helpful, especially when CI/CD is new to your environment, or your test cases do not cover edge cases.

Code quality is also assessed in a code review. Most organizations have what are known as **Organizational Definitions of Done**, or **ODoD**. Where teams have their own **Definitions of Done (DoD)**, these are the ones that apply to every team within a development organization. They are related to what are the minimum requirements for all code to be considered done. Common examples of ODoD are that "code is reviewed," "code is unit tested," and "code meets all acceptance criteria on the user story."

The purpose of ODoD is threefold:

- First, ODoD enshrines the organizational best practices for development and testing
- Second, ODoD eliminates the need to replicate these criteria across the DoD for all teams
- Third, well-written ODoD ensures that all code written within the organization meets minimum maintainability standards

ODoD, then, applies to every team, every product, and every project to increase ecosystem understanding, unification, and standards.

Additional steps to ensure best practices occur across all distributed teams are to ensure there is a living document that outlines coding conventions, best practices, and tips to avoid common pitfalls. In this living document, naming conventions and code commenting conventions need to be specified.

One of the most critical best practices is to make code review a norm. That means that code reviews are scheduled at least once per day if you are deploying code frequently. No code should be released to production without a peer-to-peer code review. CI/CD does not replace human team member efforts to ensure code quality.

When you ensure code reviews are occurring and are following best practices, it is helpful to provide your team members with training on how best to provide constructive feedback. For example, be sure the reviewers are offering complimentary feedback in partnership with corrective feedback. Corrective feedback needs to be specific and actionable. You can also offer practical advice on how to make the changes the reviewer is suggesting. Whenever possible, examples should be provided as part of the feedback process.

Remote code reviews play a pivotal role in ensuring the quality and maintainability of code bases in distributed teams. Developing strong critical analysis skills helps reviewers identify issues, evaluate code quality, and provide actionable feedback that improves both the code and the developer's skills. Streamlined review processes supported by clear standards and robust tools enable teams to conduct thorough and efficient reviews. By mastering these skills and approaches, remote teams can maintain high standards of collaboration and productivity, even in geographically dispersed setups.

Summary

Remote pair programming and code reviews are vital for maintaining high-quality software in distributed teams. By mastering collaborative coding techniques, adapting to virtual environments, and honing critical analysis skills, developers can overcome remote work challenges. Utilizing the right tools and best practices enhances productivity and fosters a strong culture of teamwork and learning. Whether tackling code collaboratively in real time or evaluating contributions critically, these practices ensure continuous improvement and project success. When these foundational elements are in place, CI/CD tools and practices can thrive, and these are our next topic for exploration.

11
Continuous Integration and Continuous Deployment (CI/CD)

Continuous Integration (CI) and **Continuous Deployment** (CD) have become essential practices in modern software development, transforming how teams deliver high-quality software at speed. CI/CD is a set of practices and tools that automate the processes of integrating code modifications, testing, building, and deploying changes. These practices align closely with Agile and DevOps methodologies, emphasizing collaboration, iterative development, and rapid delivery.

The increasing complexity of code, with distributed teams, cloud-native applications, and microservices architectures, is becoming the norm. These changes make CI/CD more critical than ever for managing complexity and ensuring smooth workflows. However, implementing CI/CD effectively requires a deep understanding of pipelines, tools, and best practices. Teams must also prioritize monitoring and feedback to continuously refine their processes.

In this chapter, we will examine what CI/CD is and why it is so important for all Scrum Teams. We will investigate the specific needs of distributed teams and best practices to apply so you can monitor and track your team's code quality practices.

In this chapter, we will cover the following main topics:

- Fundamentals of CI/CD
- Tools for CI/CD
- Best practices for CI/CD in distributed teams
- Monitoring and feedback for CI/CD processes

Whether you're a developer, operations engineer, or team lead, mastering CI/CD can enhance your ability to deliver software with confidence and consistency.

Exploring the fundamentals of CI/CD

Implementing CI/CD demonstrates a commitment to *improving the speed, quality, and reliability* of software delivery. Understanding the fundamentals of CI/CD is crucial for implementing these practices effectively. By mastering these fundamentals, teams can lay a solid foundation for automating and optimizing their software development lifecycle.

The foundational concept behind CI/CD encompasses the process of integrating code frequently and deploying it rapidly and reliably. CI is specifically about frequent code integrations and automated testing. These processes have quantifiable value for distributed teams:

- **Automating repetitive tasks** ensures integration runs smoothly and easily

- **Accelerating feedback loops** guarantees issues are identified and fixed more quickly

- **Enhancing collaboration** by providing visibility into the state of the code base continuously

Where CI is focused on CI and testing, CD involves the entire pipeline and automates the deployment of code to the production environment. A *CI/CD pipeline* automates the flow of code changes from commit to production. Each change being released to production follows a series of stages to ensure the stability and quality of the code.

> **Note**
>
> The concept of CI emerged in the early 2000s to address challenges in integrating code changes from multiple developers. It ensures that every change is automatically built and tested, identifying integration issues early in the development lifecycle. CD extends this automation, pushing code changes through to production after passing all stages of the pipeline, without human intervention. Together, CI/CD reduces time-to-market, minimizes bugs, and enhances the overall reliability of software systems.

Stages of a CI/CD pipeline:

Let's go through the following stages:

- **Source stage**: This stage is triggered when new code is committed to the version control system (e.g., Git). Tools such as GitHub, GitLab, and Bitbucket detect changes and initiate the pipeline.

- **Build stage**: This stage converts source code into executable artifacts. For compiled languages, this includes compiling the code and resolving dependencies. For interpreted languages, this involves packaging and preparing the application.

- **Test stage**: This stage runs automated tests to ensure code quality and functionality. In coding best practices, there are three types of testing that every team must complete to ensure the quality of their work. These are industry-standard best practices. Let's look into the types of tests:

  - **Unit tests**: Validate individual components

  - **Integration tests**: Check interactions between components

  - **End-to-end tests**: Verify complete workflows

- **Release stage**: This stage prepares the software for deployment by tagging releases, generating changelogs, or packaging the application into containers (e.g., Docker images).

- **Deploy stage**: This stage automatically or manually pushes the application to staging, production, or other environments. There is more than one way to release code, so deployments can use a variety of strategies to minimize risk. Here is a list of deployment strategies for you to consider. Many organizations use at least one, and sometimes more than one, of these strategies:

  - **Blue/green release**: The code deploys to a separate but identical "green" environment while the currently active environment, "blue," remains stable and users are redirected to "green" environments

  - **Canary releases**: Code changes are rolled out incrementally to a small group of users first for real-world testing before a wider rollout

  - **Rolling updates**: Code changes are small and frequent, with minimal disruption to users

When your pipeline is carefully crafted and your deployment decisions are made to minimize risks specific to your product and technical ecosystem, you will be able to deploy code globally with minimal disruption.

It does, however, take specific skills to set up your CI/CD pipeline. The first skill is to understand *pipeline configuration as code*. Modern CI/CD tools such as Jenkins, GitLab CI, and CircleCI allow pipelines to be defined using configuration files (e.g., YAML or JSON). These files specify each stage, triggers, and conditions. Additionally, the following skills will also be needed on your team to take advantage of CI/CD:

- **Scripting and automation**: Proficiency in scripting languages (e.g., Bash, Python, PowerShell) for writing custom scripts that handle specialized tasks or integrate unique tools

- **Tool and environment integration**: Setting up tools for source control (Git), build automation (Maven, Gradle), testing (JUnit, Selenium), and deployment (Kubernetes, AWS CodeDeploy)

- **Cloud and containerization skills:**

  - Familiarity with cloud providers such as AWS, Azure, or Google Cloud to enable scalable, on-demand pipelines

  - Containerization tools such as Docker for consistent runtime environments

  - Orchestration tools such as Kubernetes for managing deployments across clusters

It may not be necessary to have all these skills within your distributed team. It is, however, essential that your team members understand the fundamentals of CI/CD. Mastering the architecture and implementation of CI/CD pipelines equips teams to manage the complexities of modern software development, ensuring seamless integration, testing, and delivery. While the fundamentals of CI/CD leave some room for exploration and unique application, selecting the right tools to support your efforts will pay dividends. These tools will ensure consistency of usage and quality across your, and all other organizational teams.

Using tools for CI/CD

The success of a CI/CD pipeline depends on selecting and effectively using the right tools. With a wide range of tools available, each suited for specific workflows, understanding their features and integrations is essential for building reliable pipelines. Here, we will examine the most popular tools and their features.

Jenkins

- **Overview**: Jenkins is an open source automation server widely used for CI/CD. Its plugin-based architecture supports a variety of tasks, from simple builds to complex pipelines.

- **Key features**:

  - Supports hundreds of plugins for integrations with other tools.

  - Allows pipeline scripting using a Groovy-based Jenkinsfile.

  - Scalable with distributed builds across multiple nodes.

- **When to use**: Ideal for teams requiring extensive customization and open source flexibility.

GitHub Actions

- **Overview**: Integrated into GitHub, GitHub Actions automates workflows directly within the repository.

- **Key features**:

  - YAML-based configuration is used for simple readability into native data structures.

  - Deep integration with GitHub "pull requests" and issues so there is a single source of truth for collaboration and troubleshooting.

  - Pre-built actions in the GitHub marketplace so your team can download and use pre-written code snippets for common tasks, thus saving you time.

- **When to use**: Best for teams already using GitHub as their primary version control system.

GitLab CI/CD

- **Overview**: GitLab provides a fully integrated CI/CD solution within its DevOps platform.

- **Key features**:

  - Native support for Docker and Kubernetes to establish a complete ecosystem for containerized development.

  - YAML-based pipeline configuration for ease of use in native data structures.

  - Built-in monitoring and analytics to help you see into the CI/CD pipeline for process transparency.

- **When to use**: Excellent for teams leveraging GitLab for source control and project management.

CircleCI

- **Overview**: CircleCI is a cloud-native CI/CD tool with a focus on speed and scalability.

- **Key features**:

  - Optimized for containerized and cloud-based environments, making it highly adaptable for modern development workflows.

  - Pay-per-use pricing for cost efficiency by allowing users to pay only for the resources they consume.

  - Extensive caching for faster builds and improved overall efficiency.

- **When to use**: Suitable for cloud-first teams with a focus on rapid iteration.

Other notable tools

- **Travis CI**: Simplified CI/CD for open source projects.

- **Azure DevOps Pipelines**: Seamless integration with Microsoft Azure services.

- **Bitbucket Pipelines**: CI/CD for teams using Bitbucket repositories.

Your team is unlikely to be the team that determines which CI/CD tools are used in your organization. Knowing the pros and cons of each toolset can help your team effectively use the tools that are in place. While not all tools are created equal, your team will need to use the tool that has been designated. Experience has shown that, while not all tools are created equal, they all share the same claims to aiding in team efficiency and improved code quality.

Exploring the efficiency tools can provide

Your team members will need to understand the toolset used in your organization. Further, they will need to understand how to set up pipelines for your product, including the stages, triggers, and conditions that move code. One of the key elements for your team to grasp is integrating tools into their workflows, including the following:

- **Source control integration**:

  - You can seamlessly connect CI/CD tools with repositories (e.g., GitHub, GitLab, Bitbucket) to trigger pipelines on events such as commits or pull requests. This tight integration improves the efficiency of the team.

  - Examples: GitHub Actions for GitHub repositories, Bitbucket Pipelines for Bitbucket

- **Testing tool integration**:

  - You can get further by incorporating testing frameworks such as JUnit, Selenium, or Cypress into the pipeline to automate unit, integration, and end-to-end tests. This type of integrated testing can add significant time savings in getting your code into the hands of your users.

- **Monitoring and deployment tools**:

  - Integrating monitoring tools such as Prometheus, Grafana, or Datadog can monitor pipeline performance and deployment environments. The efficiency gained here is in the transparency you'll have if anything goes wrong in your pipeline.

  - Kubernetes and Terraform for infrastructure orchestration.

So that your team functions efficiently and skillfully with your tool suite, they will need to learn and master *Tool-Specific Configuration, Environment Setup and Integration, and Workflow Optimization*.

By choosing the right tools and gaining proficiency in their usage, teams can design and execute efficient CI/CD pipelines that integrate seamlessly with their existing workflows, enhancing productivity and software quality.

Best practices for CI/CD in distributed teams

While CI/CD practices offer a powerful way to streamline software development, implementing these practices effectively in distributed teams requires additional strategies to address challenges such as communication barriers, time zone differences, and inconsistent environments. This section outlines the best practices for CI/CD in distributed teams, focusing on workflow optimization and ensuring security and compliance.

Optimizing workflows

Basic best practices for coding apply to distributed teams. Unit testing, code review, and proper branching strategies are even more important for distributed teams. Your team is also facing additional challenges due to its global footprint. One of the critical elements for your team is to *streamline their collaboration*.

We have already assessed and offered tools for doing this. There are simply a few more things to consider for successful CI/CD implementation:

- **Asynchronous communication**: Adopt tools such as Slack, Microsoft Teams, and Jira for asynchronous updates, ensuring that team members in different time zones can stay informed about pipeline statuses and deployments. This approach minimizes disruptions, allows for flexible work schedules, and ensures that critical information is accessible without requiring immediate responses.

- **Scheduled builds and tests**: Configure pipelines to trigger builds and tests during overlapping hours, allowing for faster feedback loops. This scheduling strategy ensures that team members are available to address issues promptly, reducing delays caused by waiting for responses from geographically dispersed teams.

- **Automated notifications**: Use integrations to notify teams about pipeline progress or failures in real time, reducing delays caused by a lack of awareness. By reducing delays due to a lack of awareness, these alerts enable quicker troubleshooting and resolution of issues, ultimately improving deployment speed and reliability.

These best practices will streamline and strengthen the team's collaboration. The next set of best practices are specific to *version control and code review practices*:

- **Branching strategies**: Use effective version control strategies such as Git Flow or trunk-based development. These approaches help minimize merge conflicts and maintain a clean history of changes.

  - **Git Flow**: Ideal for teams working on multiple features or releases concurrently.

  - **Trunk-based development**: Best for teams that favor rapid integration and smaller changes.

- **Automated code reviews**: Implement tools such as CodeClimate or SonarQube to automate the review process, ensuring consistent quality without the need for manual reviews at all hours.

- **Pull request templates**: Standardize pull requests with templates to ensure clarity in communication and consistency in quality checks.

Version control, code reviews, and automation help maintain consistency in code. Another best practice is to look for and reduce bottlenecks. Bottlenecks can be caused by coding mistakes or poor logical design. The impact is that you may see increased load time, increased downtime, and increased user frustration. There are specific *tools and techniques for reducing bottlenecks*:

- **Parallelized builds**: Use CI/CD tools that support parallelization to run builds and tests simultaneously, reducing total pipeline runtime. By distributing workloads across different execution nodes, teams can detect issues earlier in the development cycle, minimize wait times, and accelerate feedback loops. This approach is particularly beneficial for large-scale applications with extensive test suites.

- **Caching mechanisms**: Implement caching for dependencies, containers, and test results to avoid rebuilding or retesting redundant components. By storing frequently used resources, caching reduces network and compute overhead, speeds up subsequent builds, and enhances consistency across runs. Efficient caching strategies can drastically cut down setup times and optimize resource utilization.

- **Pipeline as code**: Define pipelines declaratively (e.g., YAML) to standardize workflows across team members and repositories. This approach enhances collaboration by allowing developers to manage pipeline configurations as part of the code base, making it easier to track changes, automate processes, and enforce best practices. Additionally, treating pipelines as code enables better scalability and maintainability, as updates and improvements can be applied consistently across multiple projects.

When you implement these best practices with your team, you will gain higher quality code, reduced user frustration, and continuously stable deployments. These practices specifically address the Agile principle of satisfying the customer through early and continuous delivery of valuable software.

Ensuring security and compliance

As you can see, CI/CD is a huge asset for distributed teams. There are, of course, some risks that will need to be managed. Applying security and compliance best practices to your CI/CD environment will prevent attackers from injecting malicious code or creating backdoors that can cause data loss and system compromise.

The first best practice to incorporate is to *secure pipeline configurations* using the following:

- **Credential management**: Use "secret management tools" (e.g., HashiCorp Vault, AWS Secrets Manager) to securely store and retrieve sensitive information such as API keys and database credentials during pipeline execution. These tools make it highly unlikely that key system logins and passwords can be hacked.

- **Access controls**: Enforce **role-based access control** (**RBAC**) to restrict who can modify pipeline configurations or trigger deployments.

Next, you will need to ensure you *incorporate security scans into pipelines*. There is more than one way to do so, and some options are as follows:

- **Static Application Security Testing** (**SAST**): Integrate tools such as SonarQube, Checkmarx, or Veracode to scan source code for vulnerabilities during the build stage.

- **Dynamic Application Security Testing** (**DAST**): Use tools such as OWASP ZAP or Burp Suite to test running applications for vulnerabilities.

- **Dependency scanning**: Incorporate tools such as Dependabot or Snyk to identify and mitigate vulnerabilities in third-party libraries.

Another best practice to implement is ensuring *compliance and data privacy* are applied throughout the development and CI/CD environments. This includes the following:

- **Audit trails**: Enable logging for all pipeline activities to maintain a clear record of who made changes, when, and why. This is crucial for compliance with regulations such as **General Data Protection Regulations** (**GDPR**), **Health Insurance Portability and Accountability Act** (**HIPAA**), and **System and Organization Controls** (**SOC 2**).

- **Compliance gates**: Add automated checks in the pipeline to ensure compliance with organizational or regulatory standards. For instance, enforce code coverage thresholds or verify the presence of security headers in web applications.

One of the most difficult best practices to maintain on globally distributed teams is consistency. *Maintaining consistency in distributed environments* is essential to the successful use of CI/CD. Tools can help with this:

- **Environment as code**: Use tools such as Terraform or Ansible to define infrastructure configurations programmatically, ensuring consistent environments across development, staging, and production.

- **Containerization**: Leverage Docker to create portable and reproducible environments, minimizing discrepancies between developers' machines and deployment environments.

Consistency will also require *regular audits* of the team's work and processes. This can be done within the team or, ideally, within the larger technology department to ensure unbiased results. You will need to partner with the technology department leadership to define best practices and cadence for audits.

By adopting these best practices, distributed teams can overcome challenges such as asynchronous collaboration, inconsistent environments, and security concerns. Optimized workflows, secure pipelines, and compliance measures ensure that CI/CD processes are robust, scalable, and effective, enabling distributed teams to deliver high-quality software consistently. These strategies are essential for maintaining productivity and alignment across geographical and cultural boundaries.

Monitoring and feedback for CI/CD processes

CI/CD pipelines are not static entities; they require ongoing monitoring and feedback to ensure their effectiveness and reliability. Monitoring CI/CD processes provides visibility into pipeline performance, helping teams identify bottlenecks, failures, and inefficiencies. Feedback loops ensure continuous improvement, allowing teams to refine workflows based on real-time data and developer input. Let us examine the importance of continuous monitoring and structured feedback, the tools used for these purposes, and strategies for leveraging insights to optimize CI/CD workflows.

The first step in maintaining the integrity of your CI/CD processes is *continuous monitoring*. Monitoring ensures that failures in builds, tests, or deployments are identified and resolved quickly, minimizing downtime.

Regular tracking of pipeline performance (e.g., build times, test coverage) helps teams optimize processes and reduce unnecessary delays, thus *ensuring pipeline efficiency*. Finally, monitoring ensures that deployments are consistent and free from issues, reducing the likelihood of introducing bugs into production; this is simply known as **maintaining deployment stability**. When your deployments are stable, other teams and your customers will trust the product you are releasing.

There are, of course, tools for monitoring your CI/CD pipelines and their performance. Many CI/CD platforms, such as GitLab, Jenkins, and CircleCI offer built-in analytics for tracking pipeline health, success rates, and average runtimes. Verify what built-in tools are available for monitoring in CI/CD platforms. Then, be sure to *set up alerts and notifications*. Core notifications to turn on include the following:

- **Failure notifications**: Configure tools to alert team members when pipelines fail, ensuring rapid response
- **Performance threshold alerts**: Set thresholds for metrics such as build time, test coverage, or deployment frequency to catch deviations from expected norms
- **Integration with communication tools**: Use Slack, Microsoft Teams, or email notifications for instant updates on pipeline status

Simply implementing monitoring and alerts is only the beginning of mastering your CI/CD pipelines. The next step is to turn these feedback points into opportunities for continuous improvement.

Feedback loops and continuous improvement

There are two primary ways to capture feedback on your CI/CD workflows. The first is to *collect developer feedback* on the workflows. Their insights will help you identify pipeline bottlenecks and inefficiencies. The most common methods for gathering this feedback are through *regular Retrospectives* and *surveys* to capture pain points and suggestions.

The second way is to *use metrics* to inform your improvement targets. There are key metrics you should be tracking and against which targets are set. The metrics you need to track include the following:

- **Mean Time to Recovery (MTTR)**: The average time to fix a pipeline failure

- **Deployment frequency**: How often code is successfully deployed to production

- **Lead time for changes**: The time from code commit to deployment

- **Change failure rate**: The percentage of deployments that cause issues in production

These metrics, in partnership with the developer feedback you collect, will help you to establish a top-notch CI/CD ecosystem. Additionally, it will further deepen the *culture of continuous improvement* you are striving to attain.

Agile values team *empowerment and self-organization* regarding their work. When you encourage your developers to suggest changes to pipelines and workflows, you teach them to self-organize and empower them to make decisions that will benefit the product.

Monitoring and feedback are crucial for maintaining effective CI/CD processes. Continuous monitoring ensures pipeline stability and performance, while structured feedback loops provide actionable insights for improvement. Together, monitoring and feedback foster a culture of continuous improvement, ensuring that CI/CD processes remain agile, efficient, and reliable.

As we come to the end of this chapter, here is a diagram to give you a visual overview of the CI/CD pipeline.

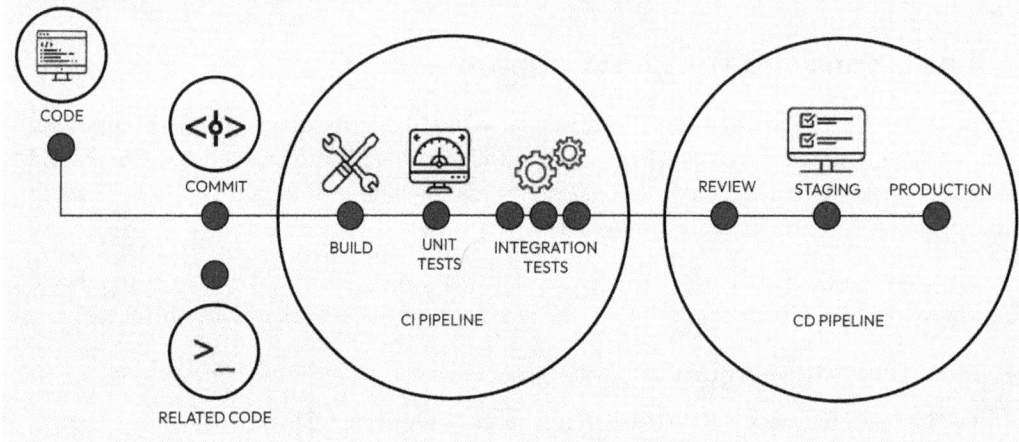

Figure 11.1 – End-to-End CI/CD Pipeline Overview

As you can see from the diagram, it's easiest to consider the segments of Continuous Integration as a whole and Continuous Deployment as an interrelated, yet separate whole. Each aspect will need to be thoughtfully designed and carefully interconnected to create a cohesive development environment.

Summary

This chapter explored the essential practices, tools, and strategies of Continuous Integration (CI) and Continuous Deployment (CD), which are critical for modern software development. Starting with the fundamentals, we examined how CI/CD pipelines automate the integration, testing, and deployment of code, enabling faster and more reliable software delivery. Key concepts such as pipeline architecture, stages, and the skills required for setup were detailed, emphasizing the importance of automation and consistency.

For distributed teams, best practices such as asynchronous communication, secure configurations, and compliance checks ensure that CI/CD processes remain efficient and secure across diverse environments. Finally, we emphasized the importance of monitoring and feedback in CI/CD. Real-time monitoring tools and well-defined metrics help track pipeline performance and detect issues early, while feedback loops enable continuous improvement. Together, these practices ensure that CI/CD workflows remain robust, scalable, and aligned with organizational goals.

By implementing the principles and practices discussed in this chapter, teams can leverage CI/CD to achieve faster development cycles, higher-quality releases, and improved collaboration, delivering better software to users. These best practices form the foundation for maintaining full security and compliance. In our next chapter, we will take a deep dive into the ideal state of security and compliance for distributed teams.

12

Security and Compliance in Remote Work

Driven by technological advancements and the growing demand for flexible work arrangements, remote work has become a cornerstone of modern business operations. However, this shift introduces unique challenges, particularly in the realms of security and compliance. Companies must adapt their strategies to protect sensitive data, ensure regulatory adherence, and foster a culture of awareness among remote teams. This chapter explores the critical nature of security and compliance in remote work, offering actionable insights and best practices to help organizations navigate this evolving landscape.

In this chapter, we will explore these topics:

- Understanding security risks in remote work
- Implementing robust security protocols
- Compliance with data protection regulations
- Security awareness for remote teams

Understanding security risks in remote work

Remote work environments often lack the controlled security measures present in traditional office settings. Employees may use unsecured networks, personal devices, or weak passwords, increasing the risk of **unauthorized access and data breaches**. Attack vectors such as phishing emails, malware, and ransomware campaigns further compound the risk. **Insider threats,** whether intentional or accidental, pose a significant risk. Employees may mishandle sensitive information, lose devices containing corporate data, or intentionally misuse their access rights. These risks are exacerbated in remote setups where oversight is limited.

Collaboration tools are essential for distributed teams. These tools, such as video conferencing platforms (such as Zoom), file-sharing applications (such as SharePoint and Confluence), and messaging apps (such as Teams or Slack) are essential for remote work. However, they can introduce vulnerabilities if they are insecure, leading to eavesdropping, data leakage, or unauthorized sharing of confidential information.

Finally, organizations operating in regulated industries face additional risks related to their distributed teams. Compliance with data protection laws such as **General Data Protection Regulations (GDPR)**, **Health Insurance Portability and Accountability Act (HIPAA)**, and the **California Consumer Privacy Act (CCPA)** is gaining more focus as hackers become more sophisticated in their attacks. Failure to meet these regulations can result in hefty fines, reputational damage, and legal implications.

Now that we understand the gravity of these risks, exacerbated by team distribution and less direct oversight, we must examine how best to mitigate our organizational risks.

Implementing robust security protocols

As with all technologies, one solution does not fit all. The same is true in the discussion of security protocols. Beginning with a definition, a **security protocol** is a sequence of operations that ensures cybersecurity. There are many ways to ensure cybersecurity, and the most secure organizations are ones that use more than one protocol.

The first protocol to tackle is to establish a well-defined framework to protect sensitive data. There are legal requirements for some data, particularly related to personal information and financial transactions. Beyond that, there is the simple fact of maintaining trade secrets for your organization. The ultimate goal is to protect the information from unauthorized access and maintain confidentiality.

The distributed teams in your organization use a combination of highly complex technology. They are regularly engaged in online activities and, by definition, collaborate in cyberspace. Further, it is rare to find an employee who does not check their social media or personal email from their work device. Knowing this, cybercriminals have taken to these avenues to access your network, your data, and your trade secrets.

Security protocols protect sensitive data and systems by verifying the identity of users and devices that are attempting access. Part of establishing and enforcing security protocols includes the following types of security measures.

Establishing secure connections

Distributed teams need reliable network connectivity to be productive. Beyond that basic need, organizations must enforce the use of **Virtual Private Networks (VPNs)** to encrypt internet traffic and protect remote workers from cyber threats. **Multi-Factor Authentication (MFA)** should also be a standard practice to add an extra layer of security.

Device management

Some organizations supply their remote workers with a laptop on which they connect to the organization and complete their work. This provides an extra layer of security in that the organization can guarantee the minimum viable security configuration consistently. Additionally, using **Mobile Device Management** (**MDM**) solutions can ensure that devices used for work maintain security standards. This includes enabling remote wiping capabilities, where the hard drive of a lost or stolen laptop is erased of all data that is stored locally.

Regular software updates and patching

The longer an application or system is available in the marketplace, the more likely it is that bad actors have focused their efforts on hacking it. Software companies are continuously searching for an angle through which to access sensitive information. Keeping systems and applications *current with security patches and updates* is crucial for addressing known vulnerabilities. Organizations should establish automated patch management processes to ensure all devices used by remote workers are secure. Ideally, these will align with the non-working hours of your individual team members. If these updates are intrusive for your team members, act immediately to adjust the timing of the automated patching.

Data encryption

Encryption, or changing readable text into an unreadable format, is one of the most effective security measures to take. The data your team uses exists in one of two states. In one state, the data is "at rest," or being stored in a data repository. The other state, "in transit," means that your data is being moved from one repository to another or is actively being used by your consumer.

Corporate policies guiding data encryption should cover both states of being for your data. In partnership with secure file-sharing options, such as Confluence, Teams, or Google Docs, organizations can further expand their security profile. Organizations must always discourage or prevent the use of personal email accounts for work-related communications. Once a file leaves the boundaries of the organization's ecosystem, its security cannot be guaranteed.

Endpoint security solutions

Endpoint security refers to security on the device where the work is being done. Security for these devices, endpoints, is a crucial prevention mechanism. This class of security includes antivirus software and intrusion detection systems. These applications must be deployed to protect remote workers' devices. The organizational policy could be that the endpoint being used is supplied by the organization, or that if a personal device is being used, it must comply with security standards. If you are unsure which policy or policies are in place, confirm with your security compliance office.

As the leader of a distributed team, you need to be aware of the security policies in place and your role in enforcing them. During meetings and daily interactions with your team members, you may hear of a security gap that must be addressed. From this perspective, you are the closest leader to ensuring the security of your systems and data.

For example, many organizations have implemented MFA (Multi-Factor Authentication). MFA is a security enhancement that requires users to provide multiple verification methods, or factors, to access a system or account. This goes beyond just a password or username and typically includes something the user knows (password), something they have (physical token), or something they are (biometric data). MFA significantly strengthens security by making it harder for unauthorized users to gain access, even if one factor is compromised. As a leader of the team, it's important to understand policies like this when they are applied to your teams. Common security mistakes of remote workers

The most robust and effective security policies still rely upon your remote workforce to be effective. Here are some common mistakes frequently made by remote workers:

Mistake 1: Relying solely on their VPN (Virtual Private Network) for security: While the VPN is a powerful tool and offers excellent protection, it is ineffective if it is the only source of security. The VPN should be one part of a multi-layered approach that includes home network security and robust password requirements.

Mistake 2: Another common mistake is workers using insecure public Wi-Fi networks to connect to the office; while it might be convenient to work from the cafe, it is probably not secure. Ensuring end-to-end encryption with your VPN is a great start – demanding a password-protected private network and secure file-sharing tools are necessary.

Mistake 3: Physical security of equipment: If your remote team member's device is stolen, there is clearly a risk of data breach. More common, and more neglected, is the sharing of their device with friends and family. While those individuals may be harmless, they are not experienced in cybersecurity and may accidentally expose data or introduce malware to the device. Finally, even when working from home, if you print sensitive information, be sure to collect it from the printer immediately. When disposing of such printed information, be sure to shred and discard it securely.

Your cybersecurity plans for your distributed team should take these common mistakes into account. Being prepared with a policy, and a way to validate compliance, will do far more for corporate security than you might imagine.

Compliance with data protection regulations

While you and your team are not accountable for setting data protection policies or even establishing security protocols, you are all collectively responsible for *implementing compliance standards* and understanding why they are in place. Team members must understand the data protection regulations applicable to their operations. This includes knowing what constitutes personal or sensitive data, the legal requirements for data handling, and the penalties for non-compliance.

The basics of compliance, beyond security protocols, include implementing *privacy policies*. These policies are developed and enforced while being tailored to remote work environments. These policies must address data collection, storage, sharing, and disposal practices, ensuring compliance with relevant laws.

In some industries, there are even higher levels of security standards that need to be met. Some examples that may apply to your teams include HIPPA (Health Insurance Portability and Accountability Act) for healthcare organizations and the Sarbanes-Oxley Act (SOX) for financial organizations. Ensure that you and your teams know which, if any, industry standards will apply to them.

There are also some broad security guidelines that will apply to many teams. For example, if your company conducts business in Europe, all teams will be required to comply with the GDPR, which ensures that all European citizens' privacy rights are protected. Your teams may need to be aware of and follow these policies to ensure no exposure to your product and organization.

To ensure ongoing compliance, *periodic audits* can help organizations identify gaps and rectify them promptly. Audits should cover data access logs, device security, and employee adherence to security protocols. These audits should also cover the secure transfer of sensitive information.

Remote teams often need to share sensitive information across locations. Organizations must use *secure data transfer mechanisms* and ensure that third-party service providers also comply with data protection regulations. Security for your distributed team is an ongoing challenge. However, you can lighten your load as a leader by ensuring your team members understand what needs to be done, why, and how.

In many organizations, security training and awareness are the focus of onboarding policies and procedures. It is critical to the safety of the organization to create pathways for ongoing training and awareness refresher courses.

Security training and awareness for remote teams

Employees should receive *regular training* on recognizing phishing attempts, creating strong passwords, and safeguarding devices. Training programs should be interactive and updated regularly to address evolving threats.

A *security-first culture* involves embedding security practices into everyday work processes. This can be achieved by incentivizing secure behaviors and encouraging employees to report potential security issues without fear of retribution.

Tailored *training programs should be designed for separate roles* within the organization. In other words, role-based training is essential to ensure each person is learning what security practices are needed specifically for their job. For instance, IT personnel may need advanced training on threat detection and response, while non-technical staff require guidance on secure data handling.

For the developers on your Scrum Team, there may be additional security elements they need to build into the product. For example, coding for MFA for a customer payment portal may be a requirement for them. Additionally, specific security reviews need to be included in the team's standard code review practices.

Conducting *simulated phishing attacks* and other security drills can help employees recognize and respond to real threats. These exercises also provide valuable insights into the organization's overall security preparedness.

Summary

Security and compliance are non-negotiable in the era of remote work. By understanding the unique risks posed by distributed teams, implementing robust security protocols, adhering to data protection regulations, and fostering a culture of security awareness, organizations can mitigate threats and maintain compliance. As remote work continues to evolve, businesses must remain proactive to adapt their strategies to protect sensitive data, ensure regulatory adherence, and foster a culture of awareness among remote teams.

Now that we have explored ensuring security and technology for distributed team success, we will turn our attention back to Scrum. In the next chapter, we will examine ways in which Scrum events and artifacts can be modified to ensure distributed team success.

Part 4:
Scrum Planning and Execution

Effectively planning Scrum Releases and Sprints is challenging and distance makes this even more difficult. However, there are proven techniques to help teams overcome these challenges and successfully plan and execute the Scrum framework. In this part, you will be guided on how to adapt Sprint Planning, Daily Scrum, and Sprint Reviews with your remote teams so they will be as effective as co-located teams.

This part has the following chapters:

- *Chapter 13, Remote Sprint Planning*
- *Chapter 14, Conducting a Distributed Daily Scrum*
- *Chapter 15, Sprint Execution and Monitoring*
- *Chapter 16, Sprint Review and Retrospective*

13

Remote Sprint Planning

Now that distributed teams are the norm, the practice of remote Sprint Planning has taken center stage as a key method of ensuring team alignment and focused delivery. Scrum Teams traditionally relied upon face-to-face planning; now they must learn to rely on collaboration tools, clear communication strategies, and well-orchestrated events to plan their upcoming Sprints effectively.

In this chapter, you will learn actionable skills aligned with ensuring the success of your remote Sprint Planning. The Sprint is the central event of Scrum. Due to its importance in both product delivery and team processes, we will focus in detail on how to ensure your Sprint Planning events set the stage for all other team activities. In this chapter, we are going to cover the following main topics:

- Preparing for Sprint Planning
- Facilitating effective remote Sprint Planning
- Establishing Sprint Goals with distributed teams
- Overcoming challenges in remote Sprint Planning

Preparing for remote Sprint Planning

Successful remote **Sprint Planning** begins well in advance of the event itself. The preparation stage lays the groundwork by defining the purpose of the event, ensuring all team members understand the objectives, and creating an environment where collaboration can flourish. In a virtual context, preparation also includes selecting and mastering the right digital tools to replicate or even enhance the benefits of in-person planning sessions.

Setting the stage for a remote Sprint

Before you assemble everyone, identify why you are conducting this Sprint Planning session. You must *clarify the purpose* for your team members. Be specific about what you must achieve by the end of the planning. Even if your team members are familiar with Scrum and its events, clarifying the purpose is always an important start. Pair this with creating a *detailed agenda* for the planning session to ensure that everyone is aware of each step in the planning process.

Additionally, make sure you and your team members revisit the Product Backlog. To ensure everyone is aligned on priorities, the Product Owner should update, refine, and order the Product Backlog items so the team knows what to expect.

Again, ahead of each Sprint Planning, it can be helpful to realign everyone on the roles and responsibilities for the event:

- **Scrum Master**: Acts as the facilitator, ensuring the session follows Scrum principles and remains on track
- **Product Owner**: Clarifies backlog items, prioritizes tasks, and articulates the vision for the upcoming Sprint
- **Development Team**: Estimates stories, discusses technical constraints, and commits to achievable goals

If your role is as the Scrum Master and you are facilitating the event, you must master the remote collaboration tools that are in use during planning. These will include video conferencing platforms and work management tools at a minimum. If there is an element of design in your planning session, understand and master a remote whiteboarding tool.

Check calendars and time zones to maximize the participation of team members spanning multiple time zones. Being mindful of scheduling ensures maximum participation and minimal burnout. As you finalize your agenda and complete the scheduling, you may recognize some logistical hurdles that are challenging.

This is your chance to proactively address them before they turn into major blockers. For example, perhaps there is a mandatory, all-department meeting which conflicts with your Sprint Planning window. Recognizing this and adapting your schedule up front will save time and trouble for your team. By thoroughly preparing for remote Sprint Planning, you set the stage for a focused, efficient, and engaging session that fosters collective ownership and commitment to Sprint outcomes.

Facilitating effective remote Sprint Planning

Once the groundwork is laid, it's time to focus on the actual facilitation of the remote Sprint Planning event. Effective facilitation requires structure, interactive methods, and the ability to maintain engagement across a geographically dispersed team.

Structuring the session

As you drafted your detailed agenda, there were several elements you included. Your plan is to ensure that the team thoroughly understands the work, how the work will be done, and the effort it will take to complete the work, realistically, within the Sprint. To accomplish these goals, you will need to ensure the following are in place:

- **Time-boxing**: Typically, Sprint Planning is time-boxed to a maximum of eight hours for a one-month Sprint (and proportionally less for shorter Sprints). In a remote setting, consider breaking the session into manageable segments with short breaks.

- **Agenda and flow**: An effective agenda might include the following:

  - **Opening and overview** (Product Owner presents high-level objectives).

  - **Backlog review** (team clarifies tasks and stories). As part of this review, discussion begins around what the Sprint Goal will be; this helps the team select the correct Product Backlog items for inclusion in the Sprint.

  - **Task breakdown and estimation** (team estimates effort and clarifies interdependencies).

  - **Sprint Goal alignment** (finalizing the Sprint Goal).

  - **Wrap-up** (confirming next steps and responsibilities).

This basic, detailed agenda is a wonderful place to start. It's a great idea to share this with your Product Owner to see whether additional experts will be needed. Further, your teams may need to add more elements. For example, if your team is doing just-in-time design, you may need to add a section on some solution options to the whiteboard. The challenge with remote planning is usually not the structure or the purpose of the event; it is keeping your team members engaged for what is typically a long meeting.

Keeping the team engaged virtually

Engaging your distributed team during long meetings, such as Sprint Planning, is crucial because it maximizes the productivity of the meeting, fosters better collaboration, and encourages active participation. These things naturally lead to better decision-making, higher morale, and a more positive team dynamic. Further, engagement helps to combat the feelings of isolation often associated with distributed teams.

There are many techniques you can use to help keep team members engaged. Attention spans are shorter in remote compared to in-person meetings. So, interactive elements must occur every 10 to 15 minutes. The simplest way to encourage interactivity is to insist team members keep their video on throughout planning. This encourages making eye contact and seeing the non-verbal cues of your colleagues.

Another simple trick for you to use is to ask people questions by name. For example, if your team is assessing the completeness of a user story, you can ask a specific person what questions they might still have, based on the dialogue so far. Finally, here are some interactive elements you can incorporate into your Sprint Planning:

- **Ice-breakers and check-ins**: Begin with a quick round of personal news or a fun question to build rapport.

- **Use breakout rooms**: Split the Development Team into smaller groups for detailed discussions, then reconvene to share outcomes.

- **Encourage real-time feedback**: Use polls, chat features, and quick emoticon reactions to keep the conversation flowing.

- **Rotate facilitators**: Where possible, rotate who is leading certain discussions to maintain variety in voices.

- **Take breaks**: If your Sprint Planning event will last more than 45 minutes, ensure that you are scheduling breaks throughout the event. This will minimize the disruptions of people stepping away in a disorganized manner.

To reinforce this interactivity, it is important to check in after each element of interactivity. This ensures that you remain attuned to how your agenda is landing with team members. These insights enable you to pivot in real time if your approach is falling flat.

Driving collaboration and consensus

The goal of all Sprint Planning events is to walk away from the meeting with a detailed plan on what work will be done by the team during the coming Sprint timebox and how the team will achieve their commitment to the goal. As part of this, the facilitator needs to *drive the team to consensus* on the plan. This can be done in the following ways:

- **Focusing on transparency**: Encourage open discussion about workload, risks, and dependencies so the entire team is on the same page

- **Using visual aids and diagrams**: Show user flows, architectural diagrams, or wireframes in real time to guide the conversation and clarify requirements

- **Adopting consensus-building techniques**: Utilize techniques such as fist-to-five or dot-voting on digital boards to quickly gauge the team's stance on a decision

When you drive consensus on the team, encouraging open, honest, and challenging feedback, your team will be more likely to complete their Sprint commitment. Only your facilitation skills can help them get there, though. By mastering the art of remote facilitation, you ensure that your distributed team remains energized, aligned, and ready to tackle the next Sprint with confidence.

Establishing Sprint Goals with a distributed team

The creation of a **Sprint Goal** is the crux of Sprint Planning. A Sprint Goal is a concise, measurable statement that aligns the Scrum Team around a common purpose for the upcoming Sprint. It is representative of the coming Sprint's purpose in meeting the product vision. In remote settings, the need for a clear goal is magnified, as it unites team members who may rarely (or never) see each other in person.

Here is an example of a Sprint Goal in action. Imagine a team is working on accepting credit cards on their organization's website. Their Sprint Goal is "Enable customers to securely complete purchases on our website using a Visa credit card for payment." The team selects and refines their stories to meet this goal and the Sprint begins as planned.

During the Sprint, common distractions can derail or distract the team from this goal. Here are some examples of distractions and appropriate responses for this team:

- **New feature requests**:

  Stakeholders request adding support for PayPal or Apple Pay payments during the same Sprint.

  Sprint Goal reminder: *"We're specifically focused on enabling secure credit card payments. Let's prioritize PayPal or Apple Pay integrations in future Sprints."*

- **Design enhancements**:

  The UX/UI team wants to significantly redesign the checkout flow beyond what's needed to accept credit cards.

  Sprint Goal reminder: *"Our current Sprint focuses only on securely accepting credit card payments. Major redesigns should be scheduled separately."*

- **Technical debt or refactoring**:

  Developers spot existing code that needs refactoring or cleaning up if unrelated directly to payment processing.

  Sprint Goal reminder: *"Refactoring is important, but this Sprint is dedicated to delivering credit card functionality. Let's record these refactor items in the backlog."*

- **Urgent bug reports**:

  A bug related to another area of the website arises and seems important, but doesn't directly impact payments.

  Sprint Goal reminder: *"Unless this bug impacts secure credit card payments, let's assess its urgency and address it after completing the primary Sprint Goal."*

- **Security enhancements outside the scope:**

  Security suggestions arise that are not directly related to credit card payments (e.g., updating password policies or account security enhancements).

  Sprint Goal reminder: *"While these security enhancements are valuable, our current security efforts should focus solely on meeting credit-card processing standards (e.g., PCI compliance)."*

While these distractions are useful additions to the Product Backlog, they are not helping the team attain its Sprint Goal. The Scrum Master needs to use goal reminder statements to keep the team fully focused on meeting their Sprint Goal.

Defining clear, actionable Sprint Goal

The **Sprint Goal**, without the context of the larger product vision, will not inspire team members to commit themselves to attaining it. It can be helpful to frame each Sprint Planning event in the product vision and roadmap from which the Product Owner works. This context, then, can inspire your team members with the "why" behind the "what."

Key elements to include in your conversation around setting a Sprint Goal include the following:

- **Business value and user impact**: Link each Sprint Goal to tangible outcomes that matter to end users or stakeholders

- **Time-bound and realistic:** Ensure the goal can be feasibly achieved within the Sprint's duration without any extraordinary measures

- **Specific and measurable:** Replace vague statements (e.g., "Improve user experience") with concrete metrics or user stories (e.g., "Implement and test a new search filter feature to reduce search times by 30%")

If the Sprint Goal sounds like a SMART goal, that's because it is. Both use the same format and structure in terms of being specific, measurable, achievable, relevant, and time-bound.

Once a goal is established, the next step is to align the work toward that goal.

Aligning the team around the Sprint Goal

Sprint Goals are collaboratively defined so we can ensure that everyone understands them, why they are valuable, and how we will achieve them. As part of the *collaborative goal setting*, encourage the team to propose their ideas and concerns, fostering a sense of shared ownership.

When consensus on the goal is reached, *document the goal*. Post the Sprint Goal in a visible area in your virtual workspace (e.g., pinned in Slack, on a Jira board, etc.). After your Sprint begins, *regularly revisit the goal*. Use daily Scrums to check progress against the Sprint Goal. This small action will help maintain focus throughout the iteration.

Once the Sprint Goal is established and the work has been selected, circle back to the vision and roadmap once more. Often, in the heat of planning and designing, we stray from the original intent. Revisiting the vision and roadmap at the end of planning, then, serves as a final test of your work's applicability to the overall product vision. When the entire Scrum Team is aligned on an actionable, clearly stated Sprint Goal with specific, priority work items in support of it, they are far more likely to attain their goal and move the product forward.

Prioritizing backlog items against the goal

When selecting work for the Sprint, we will prioritize the Sprint Backlog items again, as a team. The PO has already prioritized the stories, and those priorities are based on customer desires. This next level of prioritization for the Sprint is a collaborative effort involving all team members. Here are some key considerations for this next, detailed level of planning and prioritizing:

- **Must-haves versus nice-to-haves**: Distinguish between essential tasks that directly contribute to the Sprint Goal and secondary tasks that can be deferred if time or resources run short.

  Remember that a must-have feature is one that enables the product to work. In our earlier example, a must-have feature would be a field for the entry of a credit card number. This is essential to meeting our Sprint Goal.

  In contrast, a nice-to-have feature is that users can save multiple credit card numbers for future use. While this will be nice to have in the future and can be added as a priority later, it does not directly help attain the Sprint Goal "Enable customers to securely complete purchases on our website using a Visa credit card for payment."

- **Dependency mapping**: Visualize dependencies to ensure the tasks that are critical to the Sprint Goal are addressed first.

- **Negotiating scope**: If new information arises mid-Sprint, the Scrum Team should re-evaluate whether any adjustments to the goal or scope are necessary. This scope negotiation is a key aspect of the daily Scrum. Here is a sample scenario of this negotiation in action:

  A Scrum Team is working on a Sprint Goal: "Enable customers to securely complete purchases on our website using a Visa credit card for payment."

  Midway through the Sprint (on day 5 of a 10-day Sprint), the team discovers new, critical information during their daily Scrum:

  The payment processor integration requires additional verification steps (two-factor authentication) due to recent regulatory changes. Implementing this was not originally part of the Sprint plan and could significantly increase the development effort.

Here are the steps you can take to address this information head-on and determine the best approach.

Step 1: Team discussion (transparency):

- **Developer**: "Implementing **two-factor authentication** (**2FA**) will add complexity we hadn't anticipated. It could put our original scope at risk."

- **Tester**: "Without 2FA, we won't meet regulatory compliance."

Step 2: Clarification by Product Owner (inspection):

- **Product Owner**: "Is 2FA required immediately, or can we deliver basic credit card processing now and handle 2FA in the next Sprint?"

- **Developer**: "The payment processor requires compliance immediately. Without 2FA, transactions will be declined."

Step 3: Negotiating adjustments (adaptation):

- **Scrum Master**: "Since 2FA is mandatory and impacts our Sprint Goal, let's re-evaluate our scope. Can we remove or defer any other tasks originally planned for this Sprint?"

- **Product Owner**: "Yes, we originally planned a feature to allow customers to store credit cards for future use. That was a nice-to-have. Let's defer storing payment methods to focus fully on getting a secure checkout with 2FA."

Step 4: Agreement and adjusted Sprint Goal:

- The team quickly agrees on adjusting the scope, explicitly documenting the deferred tasks.

- **Revised Sprint Goal**: "Enable users to securely complete purchases on our website using a Visa credit card for payment, including required 2FA for regulatory compliance."

Step 5: Communicate updated Sprint Goal:

- The Product Owner writes an email to the stakeholder group recapping the new information learned and the team's chosen approach. This transparently shares what is being changed and why.

- Further reinforcement of the adjustments occurs in the form of updates to the Sprint task board, team site, or other locations where team updates occur.

The outcome is that the team negotiates and adjusts their scope based on new information to remain focused on the critical goal. Lower-priority items (nice-to-haves) are deferred, maintaining clarity and ensuring successful Sprint delivery.

Overcoming challenges in remote Sprint Planning

Even with thorough preparation, robust facilitation strategies, and well-defined goals, distributed teams inevitably face hurdles during remote Sprint Planning. Understanding potential pitfalls, along with proactive problem-solving approaches, equips you to handle challenges effectively.

Common pitfalls in remote Sprint Planning and their mitigations

There are multiple challenges that will arise at some point in your distributed Scrum Team. Here are the most common pitfalls and key strategies for moving beyond them:

- **Technical glitches**: Internet outages, software failures, or platform incompatibilities can disrupt your sessions:

  Mitigation – have a plan B for technology: Have a backup platform or at least a dial-in conference option ready

- **Communication gaps**: Body language cues are limited or invisible in virtual meetings, leading to misunderstandings or a lack of engagement:

  Mitigation – structured communication protocols: Establish "rules of engagement" for speaking (e.g., raising a virtual hand) and ensure the flow of conversation is orderly

- **Time zone constraints**: Scheduling across global regions can cause teams to operate at off-peak hours, risking fatigue:

  Mitigation – asynchronous collaboration: When real-time collaboration is hard to schedule, break the planning into asynchronous tasks – such as backlog reviews and story sizing – before the main session.

- **Screen fatigue**: When team members attend long meetings without taking enough breaks, fatigue occurs and will reduce their mental acuity and ability to remain engaged:

  Mitigation – scheduled breaks: Schedule regular breaks of at least 10 minutes every hour to encourage your team to step away from their desks. Further, the 20-20-20 rule will help mitigate eyestrain (every 20 minutes, look 20 feet away, for 20 seconds) and you can build this into your agenda as well.

- **Alignment drift**: Without face-to-face social cues, people may drift off-task or lose track of the meeting's objectives:

  Mitigation – frequent summaries: The facilitator should summarize discussions at regular intervals, ensuring everyone is on the same page

It is inevitable that you will run into one or more of these pitfalls in your Sprint Planning efforts. Pre-plan your mitigation strategies and communicate early and often what those mitigations will look like. Ensure your team members have this information at their fingertips when the inevitable happens. This will ensure the least disruption possible.

Continuous improvement in remote planning

Continuous improvement does not just apply to the technical workings of your product; it also applies to the Scrum events themselves. After each Sprint planning event, there is the opportunity to gather feedback and select modifications that may improve the event and its outcomes.

Here are some ways you can improve your events:

- **Collect Retrospective feedback**: Dedicate part of your Sprint Retrospective to evaluating the effectiveness of your remote planning processes.

- **Experiment with tools and techniques**: Test new digital collaboration tools or different facilitation methods to find what resonates best with your team. For many teams, the Jira platform has proven to be instrumental in their success. Among its most used features are integrations to GitHub for real-time development tracking, plugins to enable portfolio management, and cross-team collaboration through the integration of Confluence document repositories.

- **Promote resilience and adaptability**: A culture that embraces continuous learning and flexibility will fare better in remote planning environments than those that only execute the event by rote. The following link has some simple steps you can take to help guide your team toward resilience: `https://www.indeed.com/career-advice/career-development/resilience-in-the-workplace`.

Overcoming challenges in remote Sprint planning is not about avoiding difficulties altogether – it is about systematically anticipating them, communicating transparently, and establishing a team culture that is nimble and ready to adapt.

Summary

Remote Sprint planning demands deliberate effort and discipline. It requires a heightened awareness of communication methods, time zones, and digital tools. By following the guidance set out in this chapter, you will be well equipped to lead remote Sprint planning sessions that are both productive and engaging. Your distributed Scrum Team will emerge from the planning phase with a shared vision, a tangible plan of action, and a collective sense of ownership.

All these skills boil down to remembering the following key elements:

- **Preparation is key**: Invest the time up front to ensure a smooth and purposeful session

- **Facilitate for engagement**: Leverage tools and techniques that keep the team energized and aligned

- **Clarify the Sprint Goal**: A well-defined goal is a beacon that guides the team through the iteration

- **Be ready for challenges**: Embrace problems as opportunities to innovate and evolve your approach

With these practices in place, you will transform remote Sprint Planning from a perceived obstacle into a powerful avenue for successful, outcome-driven collaboration. Now that you know what the Sprint will hold, it is time to help the team stay focused during the Sprint. In the next chapter, we will cover the techniques and strategies you will need for successful daily Scrum in a distributed environment that will keep your team on track.

14
Conducting a Distributed Daily Scrum

The Daily Scrum is a short, focused meeting designed to help an Agile team address progress on their Sprint priorities, identify challenges, and foster continuous collaboration toward the Sprint Goal. Traditionally, these meetings happen with everyone in the same physical space. However, many teams are distributed, spanning different cities, time zones, and even continents, so it is critical to adapt the Daily Scrum to accommodate remote collaboration.

In this chapter, we will dive into the art of conducting Daily Scrum meetings in a remote setting. You will learn techniques for effectively structuring the event, engaging remote team members, tracking progress and impediments, and, ultimately, adapting the Daily Scrum to keep distributed team members aligned and productive. We're going to cover the following main topics:

- Structure of the Daily Scrum
- Engaging remote team members
- Tracking progress and impediments
- Adapting the Daily Scrum for remote teams

Structure of the Daily Scrum

The structure of a Daily Scrum is a key determinant of its effectiveness. When a team is distributed, setting up the right meeting format and understanding each participant's role is crucial for keeping everyone on the same page.

Facilitating the Daily Scrum

The Daily Scrum is a time-boxed event. The Scrum guide specifies that the Daily Scrum is limited to 15 minutes. This short duration encourages focus and efficiency, preventing the meeting from devolving into lengthy problem-solving sessions. In a distributed context, a strict timebox remains critical, helping to respect differing schedules and availability.

The main goals are to inspect progress toward the Sprint Goal, plan the next 24 hours' work, and identify impediments. For remote teams, there is also a heightened focus on ensuring alignment on task specifics. For example, your technical team members will share details about which parts of the code they will be working on to ensure there is no code conflict among them.

Each team member will share their answers to the three key questions shared in the Scrum guide:

- What did I do yesterday to help achieve the Sprint Goal?
- What will I do today to help achieve the Sprint Goal?
- Do I see any impediment that prevents me or the team from meeting the Sprint Goal?

Over time, teams may evolve beyond these three questions, but they still serve as the framework for the information that must be shared every day. One thing to remember is to ensure that your team members focus their information on the Sprint Goal. Often, team members are so deeply involved in the tasks that they lose sight of the larger overall goal. It is here that the facilitator, the Scrum Master, can gently remind them of the Sprint Goal.

With teams that are distributed and there being no shared physical workspace where reminders can be visible to all, grounding the team in the Sprint Goal and progress-to-date is essential. Specifically, this means beginning the Daily Scrum with two things:

- The statement of the Sprint Goal on the team's shared workspace
- The daily burndown chart to demonstrate their progress toward the Sprint Goal

These simple steps will keep the team focused on why they're doing their work and how it is helping them to attain their collective goals.

Structuring the remote meeting

As with all meetings, the details matter. While the Daily Scrum is simple, it should not be misconceived as low value. In fact, this event is the heart of Scrum. Given that prominence, be sure to approach planning for a Daily Scrum as you would for any high-value event.

The following elements need to be planned and explicitly stated in advance:

- **Choose the right technology**: Reliable audio, video conferencing, and screen-sharing tools are a must. Zoom, Microsoft Teams, Google Meet, or similar platforms can facilitate face-to-face interactions and screen sharing for visual aids. It should always be clear to all team members where and how to join the Scrum meeting – there must be no ambiguity.

- **Set clear roles**: Typically, the Scrum Master or facilitator helps ensure that the meeting stays on track. For distributed teams, the facilitator should keep an eye on any participants experiencing connection lags or issues, ensuring everyone can speak. If the Scrum Master is unavailable, a stand-in facilitator should be identified in advance.

- **Stay strict with time**: Start on time and end on time. Since remote participants may be juggling personal or professional responsibilities in different time zones, punctuality is both courteous and necessary.

- **Capture key takeaways**: Designate someone (often the Scrum Master) to briefly log issues or action items that require follow-up, so that the Daily Scrum doesn't derail into prolonged discussions. If there are questions that need to be addressed by the team immediately, hold them until after the Scrum event. A *16th-minute* discussion can be held on the same conference link to address these small issues. This is also where a follow-up plan can be established for an impediment that was raised (e.g., who is taking the lead and what steps will be taken).

By designing an appropriate structure for the Daily Scrum, you ensure that essential information is shared quickly and effectively setting the tone for the day's work, even when team members are geographically dispersed.

Engaging remote team members

When people are physically dispersed, it is easy for them to become disengaged. A camera-off culture, background distractions, and technical hiccups can all reduce the value of the meeting. Therefore, the Daily Scrum should emphasize engagement, accountability, and open communication, and there are practical ways to accomplish this.

First, a definition of engagement is needed to ensure it means the same thing to everyone. In the context of Daily Scrum, engagement involves active listening, participation, and responsiveness. For distributed teams, engagement also includes empathy – recognizing cultural and time zone differences and fostering a psychologically safe space.

The next key element is to actually facilitate the Daily Scrum. Often, Scrum Masters allow the event to become a mindless round-robin of updates. Instead, the event needs effective facilitation to maximize both engagement and the value of the event. Here are some practical tips to use in facilitating your Daily Scrum:

- **Turn on cameras**: Encourage everyone to join with video whenever possible. Visual contact helps humanize interactions and strengthen connections.

- **Rotate the order of speakers**: Avoid always calling on participants in the same order. This helps break patterns and keeps everyone alert.

- **Use visual aids**: Simple slides, digital Kanban boards, or screen-shared Sprint boards can create a shared focus and help illustrate talking points.

- **Leverage interactive tools**: Tools such as Miro, Mural, or collaborative chat features can be used for quick polls or real-time notetaking, making remote participation more dynamic. A note of caution here is that team members need to be actively listening to each other's updates. Be selective about when these tools are needed; you may only need them in the 16th minute or follow-up sessions. However, have them at your fingertips just in case.

- **Address time zone challenges**: If your team spans multiple time zones, alternate meeting times so that the same individuals aren't always meeting outside normal hours. This demonstrates respect for all team members and builds goodwill. This point cannot be emphasized enough, especially for widely distributed teams. The timing and cycle of the Scrum meeting rotation time is something that should be collaboratively decided by the team.

As you lead your team through this process, be sure to approach each idea from the mindset of experimentation. In this way, you free your team members to work through various options until landing on the one that suits them best.

Keeping everyone engaged ensures that critical blockers are communicated early, dependencies are recognized, and overall morale and cohesion remain strong – despite geographical distance.

Tracking progress and impediments

Monitoring progress and identifying roadblocks are central to any Daily Scrum. In a distributed setting, real-time visibility into task status becomes even more important, as face-to-face hallway conversations and quick deskside check-ins are no longer an option.

In Scrum, progress tracking often involves examining the Sprint Backlog, Sprint board, burndown charts, or other team metrics. For remote teams, these tools should be easily accessible and updated in real time.

An impediment is anything that blocks or slows the team's ability to complete its work. This can range from technical issues (e.g., broken build or missing permissions) to interpersonal challenges (e.g., unresponsiveness from stakeholders). With these definitions in mind, let us look at some ways you can monitor progress and clear impediments effectively for your remote team:

- **Use a digital workboard**: Tools such as Jira, Trello, or Azure DevOps allow distributed teams to see task statuses at a glance. Color coding, custom fields, and automation rules help highlight delays or blockages.

- **Share burndown charts in real time**: Before each Daily Scrum, encourage the team to update their hours or story points remaining. Display the chart during the meeting to spot trends quickly.

- **Conduct quick syncs after the meeting**: If a particular task is lagging or a critical bug appears, a short follow-up call with the relevant team members might be necessary. This keeps the Daily Scrum short but ensures further impediment resolution happens promptly; this is often referred to as the *16th minute* when the same video conference session is used.

- **Define clear ownership**: Make sure each story or task has an owner who is responsible for providing updates. This prevents confusion about who should report on what and fosters accountability in a remote environment.

- **Escalate impediments immediately**: The Scrum Master should have a mechanism, for example, a dedicated channel or chat group, to escalate issues to the right stakeholders as soon as they are identified. Clearing impediments becomes even more critical for a remote team.

  Impediments can be impacted by the time zone challenges that team members already face. If a team member reports an impediment at 10 AM UTC to their Scrum Master in Delhi, where it is 3:30 PM, the ability of the Scrum Master to resolve the issue within their workday is limited. For this reason, having a channel for impediments, beyond the Daily Scrum, is essential. In our example, the person with the impediment may face more than 1 day's impact on their Sprint. Additionally, to speed up impediment removal, there should be an escalation process within the team.

  The Scrum Master is the first escalation point, but impediments should not stall there. The Scrum Master needs to escalate to the product owner or technical leader (for product and technical issues, respectively) within a predefined amount of time. In the unlikely case that further escalation is needed, there needs to be a predefined process and timebox for taking that next step. The key is to define these steps in advance and avoid trying to define a process while simultaneously trying to resolve an impediment.

These strategies help you track work effectively, visualize progress, and identify impediments. By implementing robust monitoring practices, your team can adapt swiftly, address impediments promptly, and maintain momentum toward the Sprint Goal.

Adapting the Daily Scrum for remote teams

Finally, though the fundamental goals of the Daily Scrum remain the same (to inspect and adapt progress, plan daily work, and surface impediments), the approach to achieving these goals can vary when the team is distributed. Adapting the Scrum event to the remote environment ensures that distance does not compromise the quality of your collaboration.

Scrum, as a framework, is lightweight and flexible enough to handle remote setups. Adaptation involves fine-tuning the event's timing, format, and facilitation style to accommodate remote realities. The purpose of the Daily Scrum is not something to fine-tune, but simply some of the tactics that will make it most valuable for your team.

As always, distributed teams might have members from diverse cultural backgrounds. Being open-minded and empathetic to different communication styles builds trust and camaraderie. Again, cultural sensitivity should be the norm for all remote teams, so this is not something to fine-tune, either.

There are, however, some tactical and practical adaptations to consider to ensure your events are as inclusive as possible. Some options for you to explore include the following:

- **Alternate meeting schedules**: As mentioned before, it is appropriate to rotate meeting times to accommodate different time zones. Keep an official team calendar to avoid confusion.

- **Dedicated communication channels**: Use Slack, Microsoft Teams, or another chat tool for instantaneous communication related to blockers. Setting up a Daily Scrum channel can help keep all relevant updates in one place.

- **Brief check-in before the meeting**: To help people arrive engaged, consider a quick check-in question ("What's your biggest accomplishment since yesterday's stand-up?") or a fun icebreaker to set a positive tone. A word of caution on this option: keep it brief and prevent it from impeding the purpose of the Scrum. If you choose to do an icebreaker, ask a question that is a one- or two-word answer and can precede the team member's Scrum update.

- **Encourage offline updates**: If a team member cannot attend due to time zone constraints, encourage them to post their updates beforehand, either via chat or a short video/audio note.

- **Focus on continuous improvement**: At your Sprint Retrospectives, gather feedback on how well the Daily Scrum is working in the remote setting. Continuously refine your approach to make the ceremony more efficient and valuable.

Through thoughtful adaptation, remote teams can maintain or even enhance the effectiveness of their Daily Scrums, leveraging digital tools and inclusive practices to keep everyone involved and informed.

Summary

Conducting Daily Scrums in a distributed environment requires a deliberate focus on engagement and progress focus. By designing a robust structure and using engagement techniques that make remote collaboration seamless, you can increase the effectiveness of the event. Further, by tracking progress diligently, you transform what could be a perfunctory meeting into a cornerstone of team alignment and productivity.

Remember, the Daily Scrum is more than just reporting progress; it is an opportunity to reinforce camaraderie, hold each other accountable, and spark early detection of challenges. With the skills outlined in this chapter, you are well equipped to champion the art of running virtual Daily Scrums that unite the team in pursuit of shared goals, no matter the distance.

Now that we have defined what the Daily Scrum does to facilitate progress reporting in the Sprint, we are going to dive into the practical processes of Sprint execution and monitoring in the next chapter.

15

Sprint Execution and Monitoring

Distributed Scrum Teams around the world are faced with new challenges in effectively executing and monitoring Sprints. No longer confined to a single physical space, remote teams must navigate time zone differences, communication barriers, and diverse cultural norms. Despite these challenges, the core principles of Scrum remain relevant, offering a framework that keeps teams focused, adaptable, and driven toward delivering high-quality products.

This chapter carefully examines the strategies for successful Sprint execution and monitoring in a remote setting. While retaining the fundamental Agile values of individuals and interactions, working software, customer collaboration, and responding to change, we are focused on distributed teams. We will explore how to effectively track tasks, evaluate the Sprint progress, adapt to changes, and maintain team morale and productivity.

In this chapter, we will cover the following main topics:

- Task monitoring for distributed teams
- Evaluating Sprint progress
- Adapting to changes during the Sprint
- Maintaining team morale and productivity

Whether you are a Scrum Master, Product Owner, or a development team member, by the end of this chapter, you will have the knowledge and tools necessary to keep your remote Sprints running smoothly and delivering optimal outcomes.

Task monitoring for distributed teams

Monitoring tasks in a distributed environment demands a blend of trust, transparency, and reliable collaboration tools. In traditional, co-located settings, team members often rely on physical Scrum boards, face-to-face Daily Scrums, or impromptu check-ins to monitor progress. For remote teams, these practices transition into virtual boards and synchronous and asynchronous communication methods. It is not enough just to have the tools; teams need to understand how to make the best use of them, combining technology with open communication to maximize transparency and collaboration.

In the Scrum framework, face-to-face communication is the preferred method of task management. With globally distributed teams, this preferred method can be more challenging to attain. Instead, there are multiple methods of task tracking that are incorporated for these teams. The focus is on task progress throughout the sprint to attain the goal and deliver as promised. All these methods demand team members be open and honest about their work and any issues they encounter, and be willing to ask for, and offer, help to their colleagues.

The importance of transparency

Transparency lies at the heart of Scrum. Everyone should have immediate, *accurate visibility* into each work item's status. When teams are spread across multiple regions and time zones, creating a unified view of progress can be challenging. Without clear visibility, certain tasks might be overlooked or duplicated.

The remote nature also raises the stakes for how effectively teams *record and share* updates. Ensuring that each user story, bug fix, or task is documented, estimated, and ready to work fosters a shared sense of accountability. Everyone knows who is working on what, and any delays or roadblocks can be identified early. Here are some ways to ensure openness for your distributed team:

- **Daily status updates in chat channels**: The Scrum Team can use a dedicated chat channel (e.g., `#daily-standup`) to post a short update each day if they are too distant to meet at Scrum time or cannot attend. In this way, even if someone cannot join the live Scrum due to time zone constraints, they can scroll through the channel and see the daily updates.

- **Public visibility of metrics and reports**: The Scrum Master can share a *Sprint Dashboard* link each morning, showing the burndown chart, completed tasks, and open issues. This dashboard can be hosted in Jira, Azure DevOps, or a custom reporting tool. In this way, team members, stakeholders, and managers can check progress without having to request one-off status reports.

- **Open access to documentation**: All requirements, user stories, and acceptance criteria can be kept in a shared Confluence space or Google Drive folder with read/write access for the team. This ensures that any remote developer or tester can refer to the most up-to-date documentation without emailing or pinging someone.

By *prioritizing transparency*, remote teams avoid hidden work, surprises, or duplication of efforts. Everyone can see and understand the progress, or lack thereof, at any given point in time. Next, let us examine the ways in which tools and techniques can help bring transparency to the forefront of all daily activities within the team.

Virtual task boards and collaboration platforms

The cornerstone of *remote Scrum task monitoring* is a robust, user-friendly digital tool that replaces the physical Scrum board. The goal is not just to track tasks but also to empower the team to collaborate effectively.

For distributed teams, *online task boards* such as Jira, Trello, or Azure DevOps become mission-critical tools. These boards allow teams to create "columns" that represent various work stages such as To Do, In Progress, In Review, and Done. Team members can "pull" tasks from one column to the next, prompting an automatic update that all can see in real time. This ensures that no matter where someone is located, they have the latest information about the Sprint progress.

When selecting a tool, consider your team's size, complexity of the product, and required integrations. For instance, if your remote developers use GitHub for version control, you may opt for a tool that integrates with GitHub to auto-populate issues. Simultaneously, if your QA uses a specific testing suite, ensuring integration or easy data export might streamline feedback loops. These are some considerations to help you select the right tool and then configure the tool so it serves the team seamlessly:

- **Selecting the right tool**: Consider where integration might be needed. For example, a software start-up chooses Jira because it integrates seamlessly with its GitHub repositories, enabling automatic updates to tasks when pull requests are merged.

- **Structuring the board**: A remote development team configures their digital board with columns labeled To Do, In Progress, Ready for Review, In QA, Blocked, and Done. Cards move from left to right, reflecting real-time status changes. This approach mirrors the physical board, making it intuitive to track each task's current state. A separate Blocked column helps highlight critical issues early.

- **Ensuring real-time updates**: When a developer moves a ticket from In Progress to Ready for Review, automated notifications can be sent to the assigned code reviewer, who might be on the other side of the globe. This process reduces delays in handoffs.

- **Using labels and filters**: A distributed QA team may use labels such as High Priority, Needs Review, or Frontend vs. Backend to categorize tasks. They then apply filters to quickly see all high-priority frontend tasks. Everyone can quickly locate the tasks relevant to them, saving time that might be spent searching or clarifying.

Through a well-structured and consistently updated task board, distributed Scrum Teams foster accountability. The digital board becomes the sole source of truth so that no matter the team member's time zone, they can log in and see exactly where things stand.

Consistent communication channels

While collaboration tools are essential, they do not replace real-time interactions. Daily Scrums, whether conducted via Zoom, Microsoft Teams, or chat huddles, help unify the day-to-day progress monitoring. During these virtual sessions, each team member shares updates, impediments, and planned tasks. It is also beneficial to adopt asynchronous communication methods, such as leaving daily updates on a shared chat channel.

Tools alone will not ensure success if the team does not communicate effectively. Since distributed teams lack spontaneous hallway chats or desk-side checks, defining how and when the team communicates is vital. Here are some methods to formalize your check-ins:

Daily Scrum (live and asynchronous):

- **Live Scrum**: The entire team (or as many as possible) joins a Zoom call at 9:00 AM UTC and answers the classic Scrum questions: "What did I accomplish yesterday," "What will I work on today?" and "What obstacles do I have?"

- **Asynchronous Scrum**: For team members in vastly different time zones, they record a quick video or post a chat message summarizing their status if they cannot attend the live call.

  This approach ensures everyone remains informed of progress without forcing those in incompatible time zones to attend meetings outside working hours.

- **Chat channels and team chat**: Use multiple channels to keep distractions down beyond the main, whole-team channel. For example, the design team may have a chat channel dedicated to discussing UI/UX tasks, while a development team has its own channel for technical work. A separate `#random` channel exists for off-topic social interactions. The benefit here is it prevents important messages from getting lost in the noise. Having a social channel helps build camaraderie and replicate water-cooler moments.

- **Scheduled and ad-hoc sync calls**: Quick, targeted discussions prevent misunderstandings, so having brief ad-hoc calls will keep people aligned. The remote nature of the team means these sync calls can happen anytime if the relevant parties agree on a time window.

- **Status emails or dashboards**: This can be set up so that, at the end of each day, an automated script compiles a quick summary of progress from the collaboration tool listing key facts such as how many tasks were moved to `Done`, how many remain in `To Do`, and any flagged dependencies, and emails it to all team members. This provides a quick overview for those who might not have time to log into the tool or attend every Scrum meeting.

Establishing and adhering to a well-defined communication plan fosters collaboration, unity, and real-time visibility. It addresses common remote work pitfalls, such as delayed feedback or overlooked tasks.

Managing bottlenecks and dependencies

A remote setting can amplify the impact of bottlenecks, as waiting times between clarifications or reviews are often longer. By monitoring tasks closely, dependencies can be flagged early, preventing a compounding effect on the entire project. Proactively identifying blockers, such as a task waiting for a code review from someone in a completely opposite time zone, allows the Scrum Master and Product Owner to prioritize these dependencies and keep the workflow smooth.

By adopting the right combination of tools and communication practices, distributed Scrum Teams can maintain real-time transparency on progress, ensuring that everyone is aware of who is doing what, when it will be done, and what to do if something goes off track. Here are some tools to help you in these efforts:

- **Dependency mapping**: The team maintains a simple "dependency matrix" in a Word Document or Google Sheet. Each task or user story is listed in a row, alongside columns indicating `Depends On` and `Blocked By`. This matrix is reviewed during backlog refinement. When it's clear which tasks rely on others, scheduling conflicts and idle wait times can be minimized.

- **Blocking signals and visual indicators**: Cards on the digital task board that are blocked can be made to turn red automatically, making them stand out. A chatbot (or Jira automation) notifies the Scrum Master whenever a card's status changes to `Blocked`. In this way, the entire team is aware of blockers and can swarm to remove them.

- **Time zone handoffs**: One method you can use is a "follow-the-sun" model where tasks are assigned following the global path of the sun. For example, a developer in India completes their shift and hands off a task to a tester in the U.S. before logging off. They record a brief video or screencast showing what was done and what remains. The tester picks up the work a few hours later, effectively creating a "follow-the-sun" model. Continuous progress across time zones can dramatically reduce wait times between activities on the same work item so that when one region sleeps, another can continue the work.

- **Escalation protocols**: When a task remains blocked for more than 24 hours, it automatically appears on a "critical issues" list. The Scrum Master or Product Owner schedules a quick meeting with the relevant stakeholders to resolve it. This technique ensures problems are addressed. A defined process ensures that the right people come together quickly to fix high-impact bottlenecks.

By focusing on dependencies and proactively unblocking tasks, remote teams maintain momentum and meet Sprint commitments. A single unresolved issue does not derail the entire Sprint because the team has established systems to identify and remedy it.

Evaluating Sprint progress

Monitoring tasks is just the first step. The next essential component is evaluating the overall Sprint progress. By keeping a pulse on metrics such as burndown charts, velocity, and team capacity, remote teams gain insight into whether they are on target to meet the Sprint Goal. They will also know when corrective actions must be taken promptly. Evaluating the Sprint's progress helps illuminate the bigger picture, allowing teams to align their efforts with business objectives and stakeholder expectations.

In remote Scrum environments, transparent and timely progress evaluation helps teams understand whether they are moving toward their Sprint Goal or veering off course. By using a combination of metrics and structured checkpoints, the team can make data-driven decisions and adjust plans before issues become critical.

Some metrics and measures are typical for all Scrum Teams. Most commonly, teams use various chart types to measure their progress against Sprint and release goals. Additionally, they track team velocity to help troubleshoot if there are process issues delaying delivery. Let's examine these in turn.

The role of burndown and burnup charts

Burndown and burnup charts are commonly used visual aids that offer rapid insights into how much work remains and how much has been completed. These charts are especially vital for remote teams where synchronous communication may be limited:

- **Burndown charts**: A typical burndown chart shows the total amount of work (in hours or story points) on the vertical axis and the days of the Sprint on the horizontal axis. Each day, the "remaining work" is plotted, ideally creating a downward slope over time. This chart also offers clues into how the team is working. Here is an example:

  - **Ideal line vs. actual line**: If the actual line is consistently above the ideal line, the team is falling behind. Conversely, if the actual line is below the ideal line, the team might be moving faster than expected or overestimating tasks.

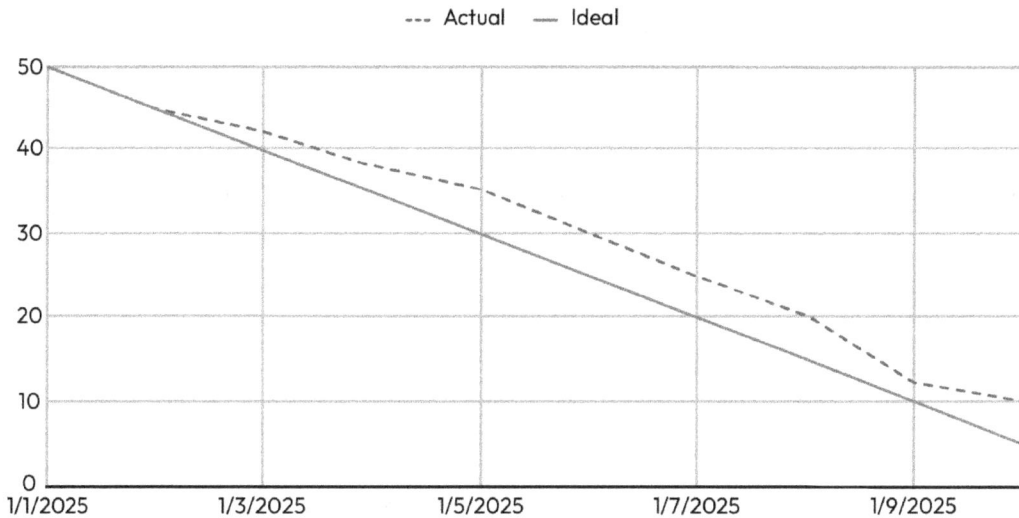

Figure 15.1 – Burndown chart

In the burndown chart in *Figure 15.1*, we see a straight line, which is the ideal progress line for this Sprint. The dotted line indicates the team's actual progress. In this case, we can see the team will not complete the Sprint commitment because the dotted progress line indicates there are still story points to complete at the end of the Sprint.

- **Troubleshooting using your burndown**: As a member of the Scrum Team, the burndown chart can be your greatest tool in troubleshooting common problems your team may face.

There are six common anti-patterns that are easily identified by simply interpreting your daily chart. Here are those anti-pattern charts and the cues they offer you to troubleshoot and realign the team:

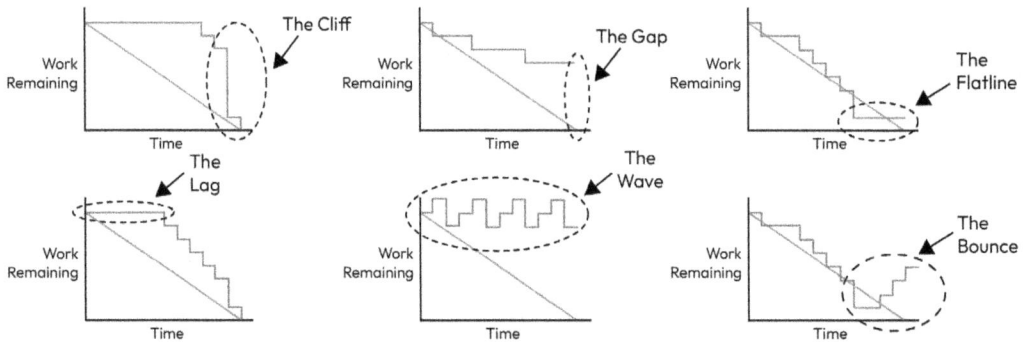

Figure 15.2 – Anti-pattern charts

- **Cliffs**: Sudden drops might indicate that multiple tasks were finished simultaneously, hinting at batch completions rather than continuous flow. Alternatively, it could indicate stories were abruptly pulled from the Sprint. Investigation is needed.

- **Lags**: A lag indicates that work doesn't begin immediately when the Sprint starts. This pattern means we need to understand what the team is working on or whether the work is sufficiently decomposed so that work can begin right away.

- **Gaps**: Work simply wasn't finished. As the leader, you will need to ask your team questions to get to the root cause. Some questions could be: Did we aim too high? Did we understand all the work to be done? Do we need to refine our work more?

- **Waves**: Work is coming in at the same pace as work completion. Questions to consider include: Is Scrum the right format for us if we have this kind of inflow? Are we setting appropriate boundaries with our stakeholders?

- **Flatlines or plateaus**: A flatline, or plateau, can mean the team is stuck or overwhelmed. Sometimes this just happens, and it's a normal aberration. However, you still need to ask questions: Did we take on too much work? Are we single-threaded in a specific skill that created a bottleneck? Could others help? Did we need a spike to investigate a story before we commit to it?

- **Bounces**: In this case, it appears that most of the Sprint work was finished, and the team started pulling in new stories. This is to be lauded as they are taking ownership of the product. Through another lens, consider whether they are working as individuals instead of as a team. Ideally, the team would collectively pull in a single story and all the work, or swarm, to complete that one additional story instead of adding several new stories.

- **Burnup charts**: While the burndown chart emphasizes "remaining work," the burnup chart tracks completed work cumulatively over time. This is used to track progress toward a Product Release Goal. This chart typically has the total scope of work on the vertical axis and the time, usually Sprints, on the horizontal axis. A burnup chart makes it easier to see whether and how the scope is changing. If new tasks are added, the total scope line adjusts upward, making it clear that more work has been introduced.

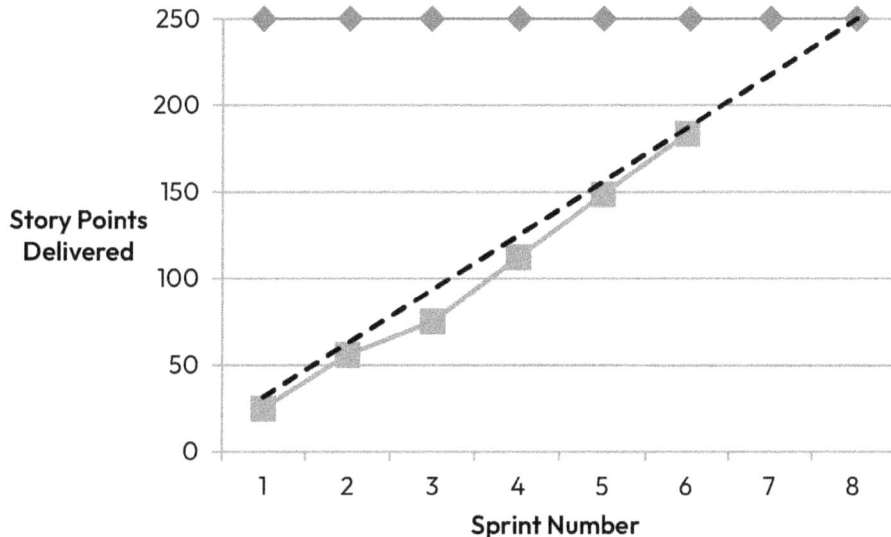

Figure 15.3 – Burnup chart

This burnup chart shows a team's progress over the first six of eight planned Sprints. The top line, with diamonds, is the total scope line. The line with squares is the actual progress line of work completed, while the dashed line reflects the ideal progress for this effort. In this case, the team is right on track.

In both cases, charts must be updated daily (often automated by tools such as Jira or Azure DevOps). These real-time visuals ensure a shared understanding of the Sprint's status, enabling remote team members to course-correct quickly without waiting for a formal meeting.

Velocity tracking

Velocity is a historical measure indicating how many story points, or another standardized measurement, a team completes during a Sprint. Tracking velocity across several Sprints helps predict future capacity and shapes the Product Owner's planning for subsequent Sprints.

In a remote setting, velocity tracking becomes key to ensuring distributed teams maintain a sustainable pace. Significant fluctuations in velocity might point to communication lapses, tool inefficiencies, or unclear requirements. Monitoring velocity allows the Product Owner and Scrum Master to plan future Sprints more accurately. Let us examine how velocity can help your team in planning, through an example:

- **Capturing historical data**: To capture a good dataset, a distributed team will log their completed story points over the course of each Sprint. Taking an average of their throughput, they observe an average velocity of about 40 points per Sprint, with minor fluctuations:
  - **Consistent velocity**: Indicates the team has a stable workflow and is estimating tasks accurately
  - **Spikes or drops**: May signal external factors, such as new team members joining, changes to technology stacks, or requirements suddenly expanding

- **Using velocity for planning**: With a velocity of 40 story points per Sprint, the Product Owner plans the next Sprint with 38 points each, thus accommodating potential unknowns. If new tasks emerge, there is a slight buffer to handle them without overburdening the team. This helps the Product Owner communicate accurately with stakeholders when work might finish. It also benefits the team by avoiding overcommitment and potential burnout.

- **Caution in interpreting velocity**: In one Sprint, the team includes many small tasks (one- to two-point stories), artificially boosting the velocity number. Another Sprint has fewer but larger tasks (8- to 13-point stories), so velocity appears lower. Remember: *velocity should be seen as a trend rather than an absolute measure of productivity*. It must be contextualized with other data points (such as the complexity of tasks) for an accurate evaluation.

A final note on velocity. It is not comparable from one team to another. The backlogs and member skills of each team are unique. It must then logically follow that their velocity numbers should be viewed as standalone metrics.

Velocity is also only a tool for the team. It helps them be more accurate in their planning and helps the Product Owner with communication and expectation setting. While valuable for the teams themselves, velocity means little beyond the team and, while tempting, it should not be used to compare teams with each other.

Aligning with the Sprint Goal

A critical element in evaluating progress is measuring whether the team is working toward the agreed-upon Sprint Goal. Burndown charts and velocity show the *quantity* of work done, but alignment with the Sprint Goal speaks to the *quality and purpose* of that work.

We came out of Sprint Planning with a clear goal defined for the team to focus on during the Sprint. *Without a clear Sprint Goal, teams risk dispersing their efforts on lower-priority items.* Here are some things to do during the Sprint to ensure the team is on track to their goal:

- **Checking progress against the Goal**: Midway through the Sprint, the Scrum Master asks, *"Have we implemented at least 50% of the core sign-up features needed?"* If the answer is no, they investigate whether tasks are misaligned, blocked, or underestimated. This encourages immediate course correction if the team is veering off track.

- **Prioritizing outcome over output**: If a team has completed many tasks but none directly contributes to the Sprint Goal, it might look like the team is moving forward, but will fail in achieving the intended product outcome, the Sprint Goal. Evaluating progress means confirming that tasks bring the team closer to satisfying the Sprint Goal, not just marking things as Done.

When you add the element of continuing alignment toward the Sprint Goal, you can help your distributed team stay focused and meet its mark. Aligning, and maintaining that alignment, to the PO's Sprint Goal means you can keep that goal front-and-center throughout the Sprint timebox. Using both reviews and feedback loops, you can make this possible for your team. Let's see how.

Mid-Sprint Reviews

In addition to Daily Scrums, some remote teams find value in "mid-Sprint Reviews" or "checkpoint demos." These are shorter, informal sessions where the team shares any partially or fully completed functionality. This helps the Product Owner, and any included stakeholders, confirm that the deliverables are on track and likely to meet expectations by the end of the Sprint.

This is a proactive way to gather feedback in a remote environment. Distributed teams do not have the luxury of dropping by a teammate's desk to review progress and suggest minor modifications. Here are some tips you can apply to your own team:

- **Structure of a mid-Sprint Review**: Halfway through a two-week Sprint, the team dedicates 30 minutes to a Zoom session. In this meeting, the developers screen-share and demonstrate partially completed features to the PO and stakeholders (optional but encouraged).

   The PO checks whether the work meets the acceptance criteria so far. This helps to catch misunderstandings early, gather feedback on the design or functionality, and address obstacles before the official Sprint Review.

- **Pros and cons**: Most adaptations for distributed teams have their pros and cons; the mid-Sprint Review is no exception. Here are some pros and cons for you to balance as you consider this adaptation for your distributed team:

  Pros:

  - Early validation of work, reducing last-minute surprises.

  - Immediate feedback loop, which is crucial when team members cannot just walk over to each other's desks.

  Cons:

  - Could increase the meeting overhead. It is important to keep these sessions short and focused.

- **Corrective actions**: If the Product Owner notices user experience gaps, they can create a new user story for a future Sprint. This benefits the whole team by transparently capturing the changes immediately.

Mid-Sprint Reviews are a terrific addition to the Sprint for some teams. Carefully weigh the pros and cons before implementing this tactic. As always, be sure to share the idea with the team and get their feedback during your considerations.

Continuous feedback loop

Evaluating Sprint progress is more than just reading charts; it is about fostering a culture of continuous feedback. The Scrum Master plays a critical role in ensuring that the feedback loop is constant. This includes adjusting tasks, clarifying acceptance criteria, or escalating issues to stakeholders who can unblock the team.

Remote teams particularly benefit from iterative feedback because they must compensate for the lack of casual, in-person observation. Here are some examples of simple elements that can create a continuous feedback loop for your team:

- **Frequent Scrum syncs**: The Scrum Master uses the Daily Scrum not just to facilitate status updates but also to encourage immediate feedback. Ending the Scrum with questions such as *"Does anyone need input from the Product Owner before tomorrow?"* or *"Is there a blocker preventing a tester in another time zone from starting their work?"* can help the team make real-time adjustments and clarifications that keep tasks moving forward.

- **Team health checks**: Once a week, the team completes a quick online survey (using Microsoft Outlook, Google Forms, or a specialized app) to measure their confidence in meeting the Sprint Goal. Scores below a certain threshold trigger discussions on potential improvements. This can provide early detection of morale or alignment issues, which are critical for remote teams where signs of stress or confusion are less visible.

- **Encouraging open communication**: Team members are urged to raise concerns directly in whatever communication channel they dominantly use. For example, *"@ScrumMaster I'm stuck on the payment API integration. The documentation is unclear. Can we get help from the finance team?"* can trigger immediate escalation.

Transparent, accessible channels for voicing concerns are critical to a continuous feedback culture.

Bringing it all together

Evaluating Sprint progress goes beyond mere data collection; it is about creating a realistic picture of how close the remote team is to meeting its commitments. By leveraging metrics such as burndown or burnup charts, maintaining a consistent view of velocity, revisiting alignment with the Sprint Goal, and hosting mid-Sprint checkpoints, distributed teams gain clarity and agility. A few final tips to help drive home this section follow:

- **Combine metrics and conversations**: Automated tools provide quick status checks, but they cannot replace open discussions about risks or misunderstandings.

- **Maintain a feedback-driven culture**: Regularly capturing feedback – through daily Scrums, mid-Sprint Reviews, and team health checks – empowers remote teams to adapt in real time.

- **Focus on outcomes**: Ensure that the tasks completed genuinely support the Sprint Goal. Chart trends and velocity are indicators, but they are not the sole measures of success.

By applying these methods, remote Scrum Teams can develop a robust framework for evaluating Sprint progress, ensuring they deliver value consistently while adapting to changing circumstances.

Adapting to changes during the Sprint

Change is the only constant in a dynamic product environment, and Scrum is deliberately designed to accommodate evolving requirements and unforeseen complexities. However, in a remote setup, the margin for miscommunication around changes can be higher, so having a structured approach to adapt is vital.

First, the team members must all embrace the Scrum framework for change. Scrum promotes iterative development, which inherently embraces change. Instead of rigidly adhering to a set plan, the Product Backlog remains fluid. However, any changes introduced mid-Sprint must be handled thoughtfully to avoid derailing the team.

Usually, changes are funneled through the Product Owner, who evaluates their impact on the Sprint Goal, prioritizes them, and only then integrates them into the Sprint Backlog, if necessary.

The role of the Scrum Master in facilitating adaptations

As the master of the Scrum framework and the protector of the team, the Scrum Master has an essential role to play when changes arise. For remote teams, the Scrum Master becomes the linchpin in ensuring that the adaptation process is smooth and minimally disruptive.

The Scrum Master may schedule short "change assessment huddles" when a significant shift is proposed. In these sessions, the team can quickly gauge the feasibility of accommodating the change within the current Sprint. If a change is accepted, the Sprint Goal is updated, and any previously planned tasks that have become lower priority can be removed or moved to the Product Backlog.

Communication protocols for handling changes

With distributed teams, the biggest challenge when introducing changes is ensuring everyone understands the new priorities and tasks. Clear communication protocols, established at the formation of the team (and regularly reviewed), help immensely. Examples include the following:

- **Immediate notifications**: If the Product Owner approves a mid-Sprint change, a designated chat channel or email template is used to notify all team members.

- **Documented updates**: Updates are added to the task board, ensuring that new stories or tasks are visible in the To Do column or backlog. Comments are added to the story card to ensure all team members have visibility into what decision was made and why.

- **Short sync calls**: A quick, scheduled Zoom or Teams call ensures that no one is left out due to time zone differences.

Balancing scope and quality

Adapting to changes mid-Sprint does not mean compromising on quality. Sometimes, new tasks might require reallocating resources or deprioritizing less critical items. The Product Owner, Scrum Master, and development team collectively decide which items to shift, making sure that the overall Sprint Goal remains attainable without overburdening the team.

Embracing adaptability ensures a healthy remote work culture. When changes arise, there is no need to panic. Instead, the team has a structured, transparent way of addressing and integrating changes while continuing to deliver value predictably and maintaining alignment with the Sprint Goal.

Maintaining team morale and productivity

When executing and monitoring a Sprint for a distributed team, one aspect that is often overlooked is how to keep team members motivated and engaged. Without the physical camaraderie of an in-person office, it is easy for distributed workers to feel isolated or disconnected from the project's bigger vision. High morale translates into higher productivity, better collaboration, and more successful Sprints. Let's explore some of the ways in which this can be enabled:

- **The role of regular check-ins**: While Daily Scrums are crucial for task updates, they do not always address an individual's sense of belonging. Setting aside time for one-on-one or small group check-ins can uncover any signs of burnout, stress, or disengagement. Even brief calls for socializing, such as virtual coffee breaks, recreate the casual conversations that co-located teams often take for granted.

- **Celebrating small wins**: Scrum Teams typically celebrate big milestones during the Sprint Review or at the end of a release cycle. However, remote teams can benefit significantly from acknowledging small accomplishments throughout the Sprint. A "Kudos" chat channel or a regular "Team Shout-Out" moment during the Daily Scrum can go a long way toward reinforcing positive behavior and building team spirit.

- **Healthy work-life boundaries**: Remote work can blur the lines between personal and professional life, leading to increased stress. It is essential for the Scrum Master and team leaders to encourage healthy boundaries. Whether by setting explicit "off-hours" for different time zones or establishing guidelines that no one is expected to answer chat messages past a certain hour, creating a culture that respects personal time helps sustain long-term productivity.

- **Building trust**: In a remote Scrum environment, trust is built through consistent communication, transparency in task handling, and mutual respect for each other's time and commitments. Micromanagement is counterproductive, eroding morale by implying a lack of confidence in the team's abilities. Instead, focus on outcome-based measures: if the tasks are completed with quality on schedule, trust that the team members are managing their time effectively.

- **Continuous learning and support**: Productivity is linked to how supported and well-equipped team members feel. Encourage peer-to-peer training sessions or knowledge-sharing meetings. Provide resources for professional development, such as online courses or conference opportunities. By investing in each team member's growth, you create a supportive environment that bolsters morale and performance alike.

By prioritizing morale and engagement, you set the stage for higher productivity, better collaboration, and more successful product outcomes.

Summary

Executing and monitoring Sprints with a distributed Scrum Team introduces unique challenges, ranging from time zone differences and communication hurdles to the need for stronger, technology-driven task management. By applying the principles of Scrum effectively, distributed teams can remain transparent, proactive, and productive.

We explored four major areas to help you shepherd your team through Sprint execution, including monitoring and evaluating progress, adapting to change, and maintaining team morale and productivity.

By internalizing these strategies and focusing on the relevant skills, you are well equipped to guide your remote Scrum Team toward successful Sprint completions. Remote collaboration no longer needs to be a barrier; instead, it can become a diverse and enriching experience that drives innovation and exceptional outcomes.

Now that we have mastered the skill needed to monitor and execute our distributed team's Sprint, we will look at how we review our results and, most importantly, assess our own delivery. In the next chapter, we will look at the final Scrum events (Sprint Review and Retrospective), understanding how to adapt them for our distributed team.

16

Sprint Review and Retrospective

Scrum is a framework grounded in transparency, inspection, and adaptation. Throughout the Sprint cycle, your distributed team works tirelessly to plan, develop, and deliver increments of work. Their whole goal is satisfying stakeholders and fulfilling the product vision. The Sprint Review and Retrospective are two cornerstones of the Scrum cycle, ensuring that the product and the process both evolve in ways that benefit the customer, the team, and the organization.

For distributed teams, spanning different time zones, cultures, and communication platforms, these events are equally essential. In fact, effective remote Sprint Reviews and Retrospectives can be the difference between a team that merely delivers work and a team that continuously grows, learns, and excels.

Two of the most critical events for a Scrum Team are the Sprint Review and the Sprint Retrospective. The first event, the Sprint Review, is entirely focused on showing what they are delivering to their customers and soliciting critical feedback. This event ensures the team is delivering exactly what is needed. The second event is the only time the team focuses entirely on itself and its practices to become a higher-performing team. These events are the springboard for teams to create improved processes and learn from their mistakes.

In this chapter, we will cover the following main topics:

- Conducting effective Sprint Reviews
- Facilitating remote Retrospectives
- Actionable takeaways for continuous improvement
- Celebrating success and learning from challenges

Conducting effective Sprint Reviews

The **Sprint Review** marks the point in each Sprint when the Scrum Team and relevant stakeholders gather to inspect the latest product increment. The outcome of this inspection is the opportunity to adapt the Product Backlog with new or modified user stories to further refine the vision of the product. For distributed teams, the Sprint Review is a unique opportunity to align everyone's understanding of progress and product direction.

There are several objectives of the Sprint Review. When well facilitated, the Sprint Review will do the following:

- **Inspect the increment**: The primary function is to reveal the working product increment. This ensures transparency and provides everyone with a chance to see what was accomplished during the Sprint.

- **Gather feedback**: Stakeholders, business representatives, and team members discuss what worked, what did not, and what innovative ideas have surfaced that may influence future Sprints.

- **Adapt the roadmap**: Based on these insights, updates to the Product Backlog or roadmap can be introduced, aligning the product's vision with real-world needs.

Sprint Reviews are a balancing act of celebrating team accomplishments while remaining open to the feedback of stakeholders. This can be challenging for co-located teams and the additional challenges for remote teams need to be acknowledged and handled directly.

Overcoming distributed team challenges

In a face-to-face environment, Sprint Reviews feel natural: everyone is in the same room, the demonstrations are easy to follow, and the energy is shared. Distributed teams can face hurdles for these same events, such as connectivity issues, scheduling conflicts across time zones, and decreased visibility of body language or reactions. Here are some strategies to overcome these challenges:

- **Leverage the right tools**: Use a robust, user-friendly video conferencing platform that supports screen sharing and has reliable call quality across different regions. Tools such as Zoom, Microsoft Teams, or Google Meet can help to unify teams quickly.

- **Maintain an agenda**: A well-structured agenda helps keep the conversation focused. This is especially important in remote settings where participants can easily get distracted by emails, instant messages, or other local tasks.

- **Promote engagement**: Encourage frequent interactions by assigning roles, such as a moderator or timekeeper, and by asking direct questions. Use interactive features such as live polls or chat boxes to keep all participants actively involved.

- **Time-zone considerations**: Schedule the Sprint Review at a time that is inclusive to most, if not all, team members. Consider rotating meeting times if your team is widely distributed. One of the tactical ways in which these suggestions manifest is to test the connectivity before your Sprint Review and mitigate any issues your tests have exposed by partnering with your IT team to resolve them. As you define the roles, make sure someone is monitoring the chat and participant connectivity.

Additionally, you need to send your agenda a few days before the event. While the topics will remain the same, the details of what is covered will change with each event. Be sure to include links wherever possible so your stakeholders can be well informed before they arrive.

Finally, you can promote engagement by asking direct questions of both team members and stakeholders who are present. If critical individuals are unavailable to attend, take the additional step of meeting with them in advance to share what will be covered and allow them to ask their questions in advance.

Then, in the Review, share their questions and comments with everyone. Record the Review event and make it available to all attendees. In this manner, you ensure participation and maintain a vested interest in your product.

Best practices for remote demonstrations

Demonstrating a product increment can be challenging when people are not physically present to see the application. However, remote demonstrations can be equally engaging if approached deliberately:

- **Prepare thoroughly**: Allocate time to *rehearse the demonstration* flow. Confirm that screen-sharing or environment setups work smoothly.

- **Provide context**: Before diving into the demonstration, *articulate the goals* or user stories that this increment addresses. This helps stakeholders understand why the features matter.

- **Stay concise**: Keep the demonstration *short and focused*. Long-winded or overly technical deep dives risk losing participants' attention.

- **Encourage real-time feedback**: Ask for *immediate reactions* or *clarifications*. Designate a team member, usually the Scrum Master, to capture feedback in real time. Virtual whiteboard tools or chat rooms can help gather comments quickly, which can be discussed during or after the demonstration.

Involving stakeholders and customers

A critical part of Scrum's transparency is inviting relevant stakeholders to the Sprint Review. For distributed teams, creating a culture of inclusivity and open dialogue can build stronger customer and stakeholder relationships:

- **Extend clear, timely invitations**: Stakeholders need enough notice to attend meetings that might not align well with their schedules. Provide an agenda so they know what to expect.

- **Facilitate open communication**: Invite stakeholders to voice concerns or praise, and ensure they feel comfortable asking questions. If language barriers exist, consider providing materials in multiple languages or having bilingual team members assist.

- **Document feedback**: Make sure all feedback is captured and visible, whether through shared documents, online notes, or a project management tool. This feedback should influence the next Sprint's planning or potentially shift product direction.

By integrating these best practices, distributed teams can host effective and engaging Sprint Reviews that deliver real value and shared understanding across the globe.

Facilitating remote Retrospectives

Where the Sprint Review focuses on the product, the Retrospective zeroes in on the process. It serves as a dedicated time for the team to reflect on how they collaborated, managed tasks, and navigated the challenges they faced. Retrospectives help *reveal inefficiencies or pain points* and encourage the team to devise strategies for future improvement.

In distributed environments, the Retrospective's importance is amplified. Miscommunications can become more common, and isolation from colleagues can sometimes breed misunderstandings or duplications of effort. By proactively reflecting on these issues, the team can adjust quickly and prevent persistent problems.

Setting the stage for a remote Retrospective

Facilitating a remote Retrospective differs significantly from the traditional in-person format. Here are some elements to consider:

- **Proper timing**: Align the session so that key participants from various time zones can attend. While perfect alignment may be impossible, distribute the inconvenience evenly among team members.

- **Use collaborative tools**: Employ digital whiteboards, mind-mapping tools, or specialized Retrospective applications (e.g., Miro, Mural, etc.) to capture thoughts and ideas visually.

- **Create a psychologically safe environment**: Encourage honesty by making it clear that the Retrospective is a judgment-free zone. Emphasize that the goal is to *improve processes, not to assign blame*.

- **Establish rules and format**: Communicate how the meeting will proceed, whether you will use typical Retrospective methods such as the "Start, Stop, Continue" framework, "Glad, Sad, Mad," or any other structured technique. There are hundreds, if not thousands, of techniques to facilitate an effective Retrospective and encourage your team to dig deep in identifying issues and possible solutions. While investigating various formats, bear in mind the personalities and cultures of your team members.

Retrospective formats for distributed teams

While many Retrospective techniques apply to both co-located and remote teams, some formats excel in virtual spaces due to their simplicity and visual interactivity. The following are a few popular approaches:

- **Start, Stop, Continue**:

  - **Description**: Team members brainstorm what they think the team should start doing, stop doing, and continue doing

  - **Benefits**: Straightforward; easy to facilitate using virtual sticky notes or a shared document

  - **Tips**: Allow each category to be discussed separately, summarizing key points before moving on

- **Glad, Sad, Mad**:

  - **Description**: Participants categorize their feelings about the Sprint into what they were glad about, sad about, and mad about.

  - **Benefits**: Encourages emotional transparency and fosters empathy among distributed teams.

  - **Tips**: Prompt participants to connect emotional reactions to tangible events or outcomes. This can reveal underlying process flaws or successes.

- **Open discussion/round robin**:

  - **Description**: Each team member is given the floor (in a structured order) to share their thoughts on successes, challenges, and suggestions

  - **Benefits**: Ensures everyone's voice is heard, which is critical in distributed teams where some might be more introverted in a virtual setting

  - **Tips**: Use a timer to keep discussions focused and fair in terms of speaking time

- **Kudo cards/shoutouts**:

    - **Description**: Team members write virtual "thank you" or "kudos" to individuals or the entire group.

    - **Benefits**: Builds team morale and fosters a supportive culture, which is crucial when team members do not see each other face to face.

    - **Tips**: Designate a digital "kudos board" that remains visible even outside the Retrospective. This can serve as an ongoing morale booster.

Don't restrict yourself to using one technique repeatedly. Also, feel free to blend the various Retrospective formats to create one that perfectly suits your needs. For example, one of my teams is filled with introverts who are reluctant to speak up. For them, I like to combine the Start, Stop, Continue technique with the round-robin technique. I begin with Start and call on each person to share their ideas before moving on to the next topic and calling on each person. Thus, we get a deep examination of each idea with input from everyone.

Facilitating best practices

The role of the facilitator becomes critical in remote Retrospectives. Effective facilitation ensures that technical hiccups, lack of face-to-face interaction, and cultural differences do not derail meaningful discussion. To move from effective to excellent communication requires preparation and focus during the meeting. Many facilitators believe that having an agenda is enough for the meeting to progress smoothly, but here are some other things you need to do to level up your facilitation practices:

- **Encourage equal participation**: Watch for silence or limited engagement. Direct questions to quieter participants and politely limit those who might dominate the conversation. A gentle redirection, such as, "Thank you for that contribution, Team Member A. Let's see what someone else thinks of your idea..."

- **Manage the tools**: Double-check that everyone can connect and see shared screens or boards and understands how to interact with the tools. Do this in advance of the meeting, particularly if you are introducing a new tool or adding new attendees.

- **Maintain focus**: Use an outline or a digital board to keep the Retrospective on track. Allow for organic conversation but step in when the dialogue diverges too far from the session's goals. The Retrospective is meant to generate ideas on what can be improved. If there is a large item, such as an issue with a tool or application, that can become a topic for future solution development. Do not focus on solutions within the Retrospective. Your goal here is to get a list of items for future solutions that the team can adopt.

- **Timebox discussions**: Scrum thrives on timeboxing, and Retrospectives are no exception. Adhere to a schedule that allocates time for reflection, discussion, and action item creation.

When you level up your skills with these techniques, you will see your meetings flow efficiently, and time will not be wasted on topics beyond the scope of your agenda. Further, by maintaining that focus, managing your tools, and timeboxing your discussions, you will identify a list of other topics that need exploration and solutioning in another session.

Actionable takeaways for continuous improvement

Collecting feedback and identifying areas of improvement is only half the battle; the other half is turning these insights into concrete steps. For distributed teams, it is crucial to ensure that commitments made during the Sprint Review and Retrospective translate into future Sprints. Use these steps to ensure that your continuous improvement efforts are actionable and acted upon:

- **Create SMART action items**: Ensure tasks are **Specific, Measurable, Achievable, Relevant, and Time-bound (SMART)**. For example, "Develop a daily stand-up checklist and test it for two weeks" is more actionable than "Improve stand-up meetings."

- **Assign ownership**: Clearly define who is responsible for each action. Lack of clarity in a distributed setting often leads to missed deadlines or forgotten improvements.

- **Add to the Sprint Backlog**: Integrate these action items into the next Sprint's workload. This formalizes the commitment and ensures these improvements do not get overlooked.

When you define your Retrospective goals as action items, they are more likely to be tackled by the team. Ownership and follow-up are critical to ensure changes are defined and applied, so make sure they are visible. I like to add my Retrospective action items as a story for the future Sprint so we can collectively track our progress.

Tracking the progress of improvements

After the Review and Retrospective, it is important to follow up on the commitments you made. This not only ensures accountability but also helps your team measure the effectiveness of proposed changes:

- **Status check-ins**: Briefly revisit improvements during daily Scrums or weekly check-ins. This raises awareness and allows for course correction if something is not working; maintaining a mindset of experimentation is helpful.

- **Use visible metrics**: Dashboards, Scrum, or Kanban boards can help track the status of agreed-upon improvements. For instance, if you decided to improve code reviews, track how many pull requests underwent peer reviews.

- **Retrospective feedback loop**: In the next Retrospective, discuss what worked and what did not, and refine further if necessary. When you add your improvements to the ream Sprint board, everyone will retain focus on internal improvements, and they can be measured to reinforce and celebrate the continuous improvement of the team. In each Retrospective with my team, we review our previous change commitments to determine their effectiveness and decide whether we have sufficiently improved in that area or additional effort is required to get to our stated goal.

Using these techniques, we are creating a culture where curiosity breeds improvement, and our mindset shifts to one of continuous improvement and growth.

Adapting to evolving challenges

As your team grows or faces new challenges (changing market conditions, new technologies, or organizational restructuring), your approach to continuous improvement must also evolve:

- **Stay curious**: Encourage a growth mindset. Explore new Retrospective formats, attend webinars on remote collaboration, and stay updated on emerging collaboration tools.

- **Be flexible**: Continuous improvement is not a static concept. Be prepared to adjust your process if your distributed team's needs change.

- **Experiment and iterate**: Treat each improvement suggestion like a mini experiment. If the hypothesis proves beneficial, retain it. If not, pivot quickly.

Continuous improvement is a mindset, just like Scrum. You must commit to acting on the feedback the team identifies as areas for improvement. Assess progress on your improvement efforts and be willing to pivot whenever necessary. By carrying out these simple steps, you will emphasize continuous improvement in your team.

Celebrating success and learning from challenges

Celebrating successes is as crucial for morale as identifying improvement areas. For distributed teams, explicit recognition can be even more impactful, as remote work may otherwise lack tangible moments of shared triumph. Scrum Teams are primarily focused on delivering for our customers and improving how we work. It's easy to become so focused on delivery and improvement that we forget to recognize what we've already accomplished. Making time for formal celebration helps you guide your teams to be proud of what they've done and inspire them to do more:

- **Sprint milestone celebrations**: After particularly challenging Sprints or significant feature releases, consider a virtual team celebration. Share stories, present achievements, or even host online games.

- **Kudos boards or gratitude channels**: Keep a dedicated space where team members can acknowledge each other's efforts. This could be a Slack or Teams channel or an online whiteboard.

- **E-certificates or badges**: Offering small digital tokens of appreciation can be fun and motivating, especially if they are easy to share on social platforms or include in personal portfolios.

While the Scrum Master may facilitate more formalized celebrations, encourage team members to express thanks and congratulations to their peers frequently. When the appreciation is universal, the team will maintain high camaraderie and morale. I encourage my teams to create a channel where they can praise each other.

Additionally, I sometimes shift the focus of a Sprint Retrospective to be one of gratitude. In this case, I share with the team in advance that the Retrospective will be a "gratitude Retrospective" and encourage them to make note of the wonderful things their colleagues are achieving. This simple technique can deepen the level of trust and collaboration on your team because everyone feels seen, heard, and valued. From this safe space, your teams are better prepared for the challenges they face on a daily basis.

Documenting challenges for future reference

It is equally important to acknowledge challenges. Distributed teams benefit from having a reference of past obstacles and solutions, which can help new team members onboard faster and maintain organizational knowledge. While you may remember all the challenges your team has faced, not everyone will, and new team members will certainly not. These suggestions will help you with knowledge transfer:

- **Continuous knowledge repository**: Maintain a living document (such as a Confluence page or shared Google Doc) summarizing major challenges and how the team overcame them. This approach ensures critical insights aren't lost when team members leave or switch roles. Regular updates by multiple contributors can also surface diverse perspectives on problem-solving. Further, clearly organized and searchable information saves significant time, enabling team members to quickly locate solutions to recurring issues.

- **Common pitfalls**: Provide guidance on issues such as time-zone coordination, resource allocation, or cultural misunderstandings, so future teams can anticipate them. By documenting these common challenges, teams can proactively establish processes to minimize disruption. Understanding past pitfalls also empowers team members to recognize warning signs early and intervene before minor issues escalate. Finally, sharing experiences about navigating cultural nuances improves team cohesion and encourages inclusive collaboration.

- **Encourage transparency**: By openly sharing struggles, you foster a culture where teammates feel safe discussing and solving problems together. When leaders model transparency, it reduces the stigma around making mistakes and emphasizes growth and learning. Open communication also builds trust and mutual respect among team members, strengthening overall team performance. Furthermore, an environment of transparency supports quicker problem identification, leading to faster, more collaborative resolutions.

Scrum is a forward-facing framework that thrives on transparency and "failing fast." Do not, however, let those valuable lessons learned go undocumented and unheard by future team members. A wonderful example of failing fast is the story of Netflix and their "Qwikster" product of 2011, where they tried to split their DVD rental and streaming services into two different products. This was soundly rejected by their customers and resulted in a significant loss of customers and company value.

Netflix openly acknowledged this mistake and studied customer feedback to change their product approach. More importantly, the Netflix CEO acknowledged that there had been significant pushback on the idea within the organization, but employees were hesitant to share their concerns because the CEO was so on board with the idea.

As a result, Netflix changed their internal practices and these practices are still in place today. They adopted a practice known as *farming for dissent*, where everyone involved in major initiatives and proposals solicits candid feedback. The goal is to gain broad perspectives and, more importantly, foster a culture that values dialogue and constructive criticism. You can read about this in detail at the following link: `https://packt.link/5fttU`.

The objective, then, for your efforts in documenting challenges and root cause analysis, is to reinforce a culture of curiosity and learning from mistakes, and welcoming mistakes as pivotal points for learning and growth.

Fostering a culture of resilience and adaptation

Beyond just celebrating and documenting, the real power of effective Sprint Reviews and Retrospectives lies in how they strengthen team resilience. When people see that their feedback leads to tangible changes, then motivation and trust surge:

- **Highlight learning opportunities**: Celebrate the learning process, even if some experiments fail. Emphasize that failures are lessons in disguise, which is essential for innovation. Encourage teams to openly analyze setbacks and articulate precisely what they have learned from each unsuccessful attempt. Recognizing these experiences helps everyone understand that innovation inherently involves uncertainty, and not all paths will lead directly to success. Over time, this approach builds a culture where calculated risk-taking is encouraged, supporting continuous improvement and creative problem-solving.

- **Champion open dialogue**: Promote an atmosphere where team members from diverse backgrounds feel comfortable voicing opinions or suggestions. Make it clear that all perspectives are valued and necessary for the team's collective growth. Facilitate discussions so quieter voices feel empowered, and ensure dominant personalities do not overshadow valuable contributions from others. Provide platforms or dedicated times for reflection to ensure all ideas receive attention and consideration. By establishing psychological safety, you create a culture where candid communication becomes the norm, directly enhancing team resilience and adaptability.

- **Encourage skill development**: Through Retrospectives, identify areas where new skills are needed. Provide training or mentorship programs that empower team members to step up and grow. Clearly communicate that skill development is viewed as an investment in everyone's career path, as well as a direct benefit to the entire team's success. Foster opportunities for team members to share and teach skills to one another, building collaborative relationships and internal support networks. Regularly revisit and assess skills progression, ensuring the team's competencies evolve alongside shifting project demands and organizational goals.

With your facilitation skills and demonstration of how to turn feedback into action, you will help your team grow in their resilience.

Summary

Sprint Reviews and Retrospectives are essential for unlocking the insight and creativity of distributed Scrum Teams. Sprint Reviews focus on the product – evaluating the increment, gathering stakeholder feedback, and aligning on future direction. When interactive and transparent, these sessions help remote members stay focused on shared goals.

Retrospectives shift the focus inward on teamwork and continuous improvement. Distributed teams face unique challenges, such as communication gaps and cultural differences, making candid retrospection crucial. Using collaborative tools, varied formats, and skilled facilitation, teams can surface hidden issues and create actionable improvement plans.

By tracking actions, recognizing wins, and documenting challenges, distributed teams foster a culture of learning and growth. Celebrating achievements builds morale, while capturing lessons ensures knowledge is retained and shared.

With these practices, each Sprint becomes a stepping stone toward stronger collaboration, greater productivity, and continuous evolution. As teams evolve, they must continuously assess their toolkit to ensure they are leveraging all tools at their disposal to work smarter.

Next steps

Advanced Distributed Scrum is an essential resource designed for today's evolving workplace, where remote collaboration has become commonplace. This pragmatic guide addresses the complexities of adapting Scrum, a traditionally in-person Agile methodology, to effectively function in distributed and remote environments.

You have gained an in-depth understanding of how Scrum principles, including Backlog refinement, Sprint Planning, Daily Scrum, and Sprint Retrospectives, can be successfully adapted for remote teams. This book identifies key challenges such as miscommunication, maintaining team cohesion, and aligning teams across different time zones, offering concrete strategies to overcome these obstacles through enhanced communication techniques and clearly defined collaboration practices.

The book highlights a comprehensive range of technological tools essential for remote Scrum Teams, from robust Work Management platforms to efficient video conferencing systems, enabling teams to collaborate seamlessly despite geographic separation'. Rich with real-world case studies and practical examples, readers will discover actionable best practices and learn directly from successful organizations that have navigated distributed Scrum.

Additionally, *Advanced Distributed Scrum* emphasizes the importance of maintaining engagement, motivation, and alignment within distributed teams, providing effective solutions for overcoming feelings of isolation or disconnection that frequently challenge remote workforces. Whether you are a seasoned Scrum Master, a practitioner transitioning to remote Scrum, or a team leader responsible for managing distributed teams, this book offers valuable insights, techniques, and actionable advice to harness the full potential of Agile practices in remote settings, ensuring consistent, high-quality outcomes and strengthened team resilience.

As an immediate plan of action, you can consider the following:

- Engage in online communities or forums focused on distributed Agile practices to share experiences and gain additional insights

- Experiment with different remote collaboration tools recommended in the book to find the best fit for your team's specific needs

- Attend webinars or workshops on advanced distributed Scrum methodologies to continue expanding your knowledge

- Implement regular Retrospectives to continuously adapt and refine your distributed Scrum practices based on feedback and experiences

- Consider certification programs or advanced training courses to further enhance your professional development in distributed Agile frameworks

Appendix
Using AI to Supercharge Scrum Teams

Remote and distributed work is here to stay, and that is why it's essential to work smarter across borders and use intelligent tools to help you. Teams are collaborating across time zones, continents, and even cultures – and Scrum Teams are no exception. While the core Scrum framework provides a solid foundation for collaboration, it wasn't built with 12-hour time zone gaps and asynchronous updates in mind.

That's where AI steps in. Artificial Intelligence (AI) has started showing up in practical ways in Agile workflows. From helping teams forecast their capacity more accurately, to writing better user stories, to running smarter retrospectives, AI is becoming a quiet force multiplier for distributed Scrum Teams.

Let's take a look at how AI can help your team plan better, communicate more effectively, and make smarter decisions. We'll also explore the pitfalls: where AI can go wrong, and how to use it with human judgment, not instead of it.

Key advantages of AI for Scrum Teams

AI has already revolutionized the way the world works. Everything from automating tasks to self-driving cars and personalizing experiences has been touched by this technology. The technology is also being used to guide architecture and construction to enhance safety and shorten project timelines.

It seems reasonable then to think that AI can have significant benefits. Let's examine what AI can bring to a Scrum Team, regardless of where your team members are located:

- **Smarter Sprint Planning**

  AI tools can predict how much work your team is likely to complete, based on past performance. This is especially helpful for remote teams who don't always have live planning meetings or consistent velocity.

- **Better communication**

  Tools such as Slack bots and AI assistants can summarize daily updates, convert time-consuming threads into quick bullet points, and help teams communicate asynchronously without missing key info.

- **Backlog management**

  AI can analyze patterns in your backlog, prioritize work based on business impact, and even draft user stories from customer feedback. It's like giving your Product Owner a smart assistant.

- **Insightful Retrospectives**

  AI-driven sentiment analysis can pick up patterns in how team members are feeling, even if they don't say it outright. It helps uncover morale issues or friction early – without waiting for a crisis.

- **Time zone coordination**

  AI can schedule meetings at optimal times across distributed time zones, detect handoff delays, and flag productivity drops that might relate to scheduling misalignments.

Minimize delays, maximize delivery

A study by the **Project Management Institute** (**PMI**) found that organizations leveraging AI tools for scheduling and resource allocation experienced a 15% reduction in project delays. This is especially impactful for Agile teams operating in distributed environments.

For remote Scrum Teams, AI's predictive capabilities enable Scrum Masters and Product Owners to anticipate blockers, forecast capacity, and reassign work across time zones before issues escalate. This proactive planning helps maintain sprint cadence and increases delivery reliability, even across geographically dispersed teams.

AI also boosts communication efficiency, which is a common pain point for distributed Agile teams. Tools such as AI-powered Slackbots or virtual assistants automate routine tasks such as sharing daily standup summaries, delivering sprint progress updates, and responding to questions about task status or backlog priorities. This ensures that team members in any location have real-time access to the information they need, without waiting for synchronous meetings or manual follow-ups.

The result is a more responsive, self-organizing team that spends less time chasing information and more time delivering value. By minimizing delays caused by miscommunication and unanticipated bottlenecks, AI helps distributed Agile teams operate with greater speed, clarity, and cohesion, ultimately improving both the velocity and predictability of project outcomes.

Disadvantages and risks of AI in Agile

No tool is perfect, and AI, just like Scrum itself, is not a silver bullet that will solve all your problems. AI has its own set of potential pitfalls. Understanding the potential downsides of this tool will help you keep a watchful eye on team progress and act when needed. Here are the most common mistakes teams make when adopting AI in their Scrum.

- **Over-reliance**

  If your team starts treating AI forecasts as infallible, you risk losing critical thinking and collaboration. Remember that Scrum is about the people first; processes and tools are secondary to the team. *AI should be a guide, not a dictator.*

- **Garbage in, garbage out**

  If your backlog is a mess or your story points are wildly inconsistent, the predictions you get from AI tools will be just as unreliable. Before applying any AI tool, the team must do all the legwork required to get the backlog into an actionable state.

- **Privacy and security**

  Some AI tools require access to chat logs, documents, and codebases. If you're working in healthcare, finance, or government, this can raise serious compliance concerns. Before selecting or using any AI tool, consult with your technology and legal leadership for guidance.

- **Team trust**

  If team members don't understand how AI tools work, they may not trust recommendations. This could lead to friction, especially in a remote setting where clarity is already tough to maintain. Before using an AI tool, or the AI built into your existing tools, take the time to socialize the idea, the pros, and the cons with your team. Transparency on your part will garner trust on the team's part.

AI in action: practical uses in Scrum events

Let's walk through how AI can show up during each part of the Scrum cycle. These aren't hypothetical cases. Teams are already using AI in this way today.

Sprint Planning

Sprint Planning is the launchpad for each sprint – it's where the team aligns on the scope of work and commits to a Sprint goal. Distributed teams face challenges such as limited real-time collaboration and uncertainty about team availability, and this is where AI tools shine.

How AI help

- Forecasts how many story points the team can handle based on recent history
- Flags stories that look like outliers (too big, too vague, too risky)
- Simulates different backlog configurations and their likelihood of completion

Example:

A globally distributed fintech team uses Forecast by Tempo to plan its Sprint. The tool runs a simulation using the last 6 Sprints and recommends committing to no more than 32 story points for an 85% likelihood of success. As the team adds more stories, the AI visually shows the probability of success dropping in real time. A large API integration task is flagged as high risk based on historical overruns. The team decides to split it and delay half until the next Sprint, increasing confidence and improving focus.

Remember that AI does not select the Sprint Goal, nor does it do the act of empirical product inspection; these are still solely the domain of the team. Rather, AI lends a hand with rapid analysis and recommendations of scope.

Daily Scrum

The Daily Scrum helps the team inspect progress and adapt the plan. But in distributed teams, not everyone can join at the same time – or even every day. AI helps keep everyone aligned regardless of time zones.

How AI helps

- Summarizes team member updates from Git, Jira, and Slack
- Sends out standup summaries automatically for asynchronous contributors
- Tracks work item movement to spot blockers

Example:

A team spanning London, Mumbai, and San Francisco uses Standuply integrated with Slack. Each morning, team members asynchronously submit updates via chat. The AI summarizes everyone's input and posts a digest before the next region wakes up. When a developer skips updates for two days and commits a stall, the AI notifies the Scrum Master of a potential blocker. The issue turns out to be a failed test environment – the team resolves it a day earlier than they would have otherwise.

Sprint Review

Sprint Review is about demonstrating what was built and gathering feedback. AI can streamline preparation and help communicate outcomes to stakeholders who might not attend live.

How AI helps

- Generates release notes from pull requests and completed Jira stories
- Clusters completed work into themes for stakeholder presentations

Example:

A health tech team uses Jira Smart Commits and the ChatGPT API to draft the release summary. The AI compiles completed tickets and clusters them under themes such as "User Onboarding Enhancements" and "Security Fixes." The Product Owner copies the summary into Confluence and shares it with remote stakeholders before the demo, reducing the live meeting time by 40%. Post-demo, AI tools convert chat feedback into backlog items tagged for refinement.

Sprint Retrospective

The Sprint Retrospective is the team's opportunity to reflect and improve. In distributed teams, some voices may go unheard, or patterns may be missed. AI can surface unseen issues and enrich the quality of discussion.

How AI helps

- Clusters retro comments into common themes (e.g. "communication delays")
- Uses sentiment analysis to spot frustration or disengagement
- Suggests action items based on previous retros

Example:

A software team with members in Brazil, Germany, and South Korea uses Parabol for retros. Team members enter feedback asynchronously. The tool analyzes tone and clusters similar concerns, highlighting "delays due to unclear handoffs." The Scrum Master hadn't seen this pattern before, but it's now backed by data. The team agrees to create a standardized handoff checklist and pair developers across time zones for smoother transitions.

Backlog Refinement

Backlog Refinement ensures the Product Backlog stays ordered and ready for upcoming Sprints. For distributed teams juggling asynchronous collaboration, AI can automate prep work and guide estimation.

How AI helps

- Suggests estimates based on past similar stories
- Highlights duplicates or related backlog items
- Converts raw notes or user feedback into structured backlog items

Example:

The Product Owner of a global e-commerce team pulls in 25 new user feedback tickets from Zendesk. The team uses an AI tool to convert them into 7 structured backlog items. One story is flagged as a near-duplicate of a task logged two Sprints ago. Another has a dependency on a service not yet updated. The AI suggests an estimate based on similar tickets and recommends breaking it into two parts. What once took 3 hours of prep is now done in 30 minutes.

Using AI wisely: best practices for distributed Scrum Teams

AI is powerful, but only if used with intention. As AI becomes increasingly embedded in the Agile toolkit, the temptation to lean too heavily on its capabilities grows. But using AI wisely isn't about handing over control – it's about integrating it thoughtfully into the human-centric processes that make Scrum effective.

For distributed teams, where visibility and coordination are often strained by distance and time zones, AI can serve as a powerful enabler. Yet without care, it can just as easily introduce new blind spots, foster over-reliance, or erode team trust.

At its best, AI enhances but does not replace the essential conversations that drive Agile success. It helps surface data insights more quickly, highlight patterns we might overlook, and automate low-value tasks so people can focus on high-value work: decision-making, collaboration, and innovation. When used correctly, AI becomes a partner in clarity.

Wise usage starts with transparency. Teams should understand how AI-generated forecasts or suggestions are created and how to challenge them when needed. AI should support team self-management, not undermine it. It should offer options – not orders. Most importantly, AI must be treated as a tool for supporting agility, not controlling it.

In short, AI works best when it complements Agile values– empowering teams to inspect, adapt, and continuously improve with greater precision and speed. But it's the humans who still carry accountability.

The smart path forward isn't blindly adopting AI but deliberately integrating it into the fabric of how your teams work together. Here's how to keep your distributed team healthy and effective while bringing AI into your processes:

- **Involve the whole team**

  Don't just "install a bot" and call it a day. Talk about how the AI tool works. Let people ask questions. Transparency builds trust.

- **Use AI for Insight, not authority**

  Let the AI inform your decisions, but always make space for team judgment. Empiricism and inspect/adapt cycles still matter.

- **Protect sensitive data**

  Check your tools' privacy policies – especially if you're in a regulated industry. Avoid uploading proprietary information to AI models without proper safeguards.

- **Make outputs visible**

  Use dashboards, shared boards, or Confluence pages so everyone – regardless of time zone – can see and interact with AI-generated insights.

- **Start small**

  Pilot AI using one event (such as Sprint Planning) before rolling it out to others. Learn what works, tweak it, then expand.

AI is a partner

AI is not a replacement for team collaboration, empiricism, or the Agile mindset. AI will not replace your team or the events you need to run Scrum successfully. AI is a wonderful support tool for your team if you apply it wisely.

I have also heard that AI will, ultimately, replace Scrum Masters. From my perspective, I don't see how that is possible. Highly skilled and experienced Scrum Masters bring elements to their teams that AI cannot replace. Specifically, AI doesn't exist in the human, emotional world of high-stress projects where the robust emotional intelligence of a great Scrum Master can help the team in ways that data-driven decisions cannot: by embracing the humanity of the team and accepting their progress unconditionally.

The Scrum Master is essential and becomes even more powerful when wisely adding AI to their Scrum tool belt. AI helps remote teams stay aligned, reduce surprises, and make data-based decisions. But it only works when paired with good Agile habits: transparency, collaboration, continuous learning, and trust.

As your team grows more global and complex, let AI take on the data grunt work. This will free your team members to focus on the human stuff: solving problems, building great products, and working well together.

> **Note**
>
> If you are going to add AI to your Scrum repertoire, be sure to do so with intentional and transparent applications of AI. You are encouraged to involve everyone in AI tool adoption, keep human judgment central to decision-making, and treat AI outputs as conversation starters, not final conclusions. Best practices include starting small, protecting sensitive data, and using dashboards to promote shared understanding across time zones.
>
> Ultimately, AI serves distributed Scrum Teams best when it automates what's repetitive, clarifies what's complex, and frees humans to focus on creativity, problem-solving, and collaboration. When used wisely, AI doesn't change Scrum – it amplifies its potential.

Index

‹packt›

packtpub.com

Subscribe to our online digital library for full access to over 7,000 books and videos, as well as industry leading tools to help you plan your personal development and advance your career. For more information, please visit our website.

Why subscribe?

- Spend less time learning and more time coding with practical eBooks and Videos from over 4,000 industry professionals

- Improve your learning with Skill Plans built especially for you

- Get a free eBook or video every month

- Fully searchable for easy access to vital information

- Copy and paste, print, and bookmark content

Did you know that Packt offers eBook versions of every book published, with PDF and ePub files available? You can upgrade to the eBook version at packtpub.com and as a print book customer, you are entitled to a discount on the eBook copy. Get in touch with us at customercare@packtpub.com for more details.

At www.packtpub.com, you can also read a collection of free technical articles, sign up for a range of free newsletters, and receive exclusive discounts and offers on Packt books and eBooks.

Other Books You May Enjoy

If you enjoyed this book, you may be interested in these other books by Packt:

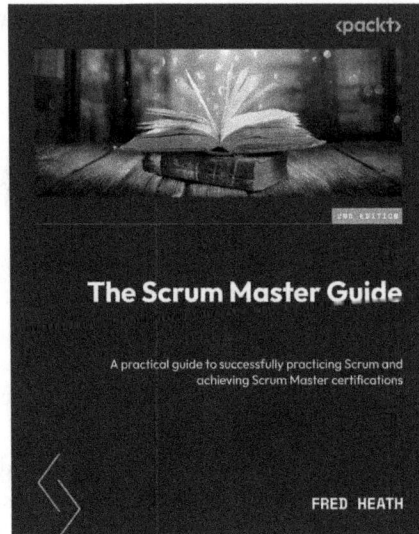

The Scrum Master Guide - Second Edition

Fred Heath

ISBN: 978-1-83588-502-4

- Understand the benefits of Agile development and the application of Scrum Values
- Discern the roles and accountabilities of Scrum Team members
- Conduct Scrum events and manage Scrum artifacts effectively
- Recognize Scrum anti-patterns and implement best practices to prevent them
- Master techniques and tools for effective planning and forecasting
- Discover when and how to provide support to the Scrum Team as a Scrum Master
- Familiarize yourself with the format of certification exams to prepare for success

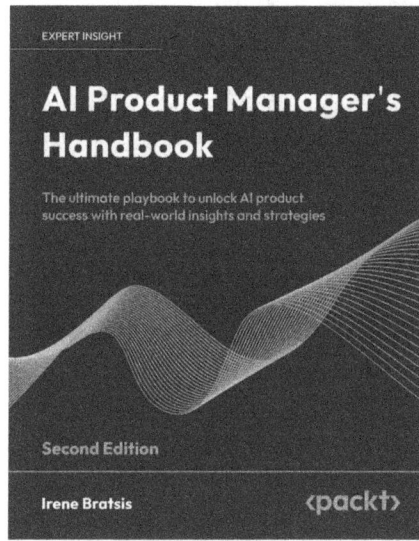

AI Product Manager's Handbook - Second Edition

Irene Bratsis

ISBN: 978-1-83588-284-9

- Plan your AI PM roadmap and navigate your career with clarity and confidence
- Gain a foundational understanding of AI/ML capabilities
- Align your product strategy, nurture your team, and navigate the ongoing challenges of cost, tech, compliance, and risk management
- Identify pitfalls and green flags for optimal commercialization
- Separate hype from reality and identify quick wins for AI enablement and GenAI
- Understand how to develop and manage both native and evolving AI products
- Benchmark product success from a holistic perspective

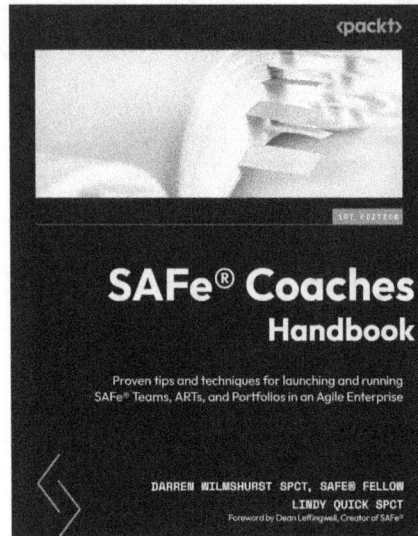

SAFe® Coaches Handbook

Darren Wilmshurst Spct, Safe® Fellow, Lindy Quick Spct

ISBN: 978-1-83921-045-7

- Discover how to set up Agile Teams to attain maximum effectiveness

- Avoid common mistakes organizations make with SAFe®

- Find out how to set up the Agile Release Train

- Discover common mistakes enterprises make that affect the success of the ART

- Understand the importance of Value Streams and learn how to work with them successfully

- Start using the best ways to measure the progress of Teams and ARTs at an Enterprise level

- Recognize the impact of successful SAFe® adoption on Enterprise strategy and organizational structure

Packt is searching for authors like you

If you're interested in becoming an author for Packt, please visit `authors.packtpub.com` and apply today. We have worked with thousands of developers and tech professionals, just like you, to help them share their insight with the global tech community. You can make a general application, apply for a specific hot topic that we are recruiting an author for, or submit your own idea.

Share Your Thoughts

Now you've finished *Advanced Distributed Scrum*, we'd love to hear your thoughts! Scan the QR code below to go straight to the Amazon review page for this book and share your feedback or leave a review on the site that you purchased it from.

`https://packt.link/r/1835468543`

Your review is important to us and the tech community and will help us make sure we're delivering excellent quality content.

Download a free PDF copy of this book

Thanks for purchasing this book!

Do you like to read on the go but are unable to carry your print books everywhere?

Is your eBook purchase not compatible with the device of your choice?

Don't worry, now with every Packt book you get a DRM-free PDF version of that book at no cost.

Read anywhere, any place, on any device. Search, copy, and paste code from your favorite technical books directly into your application.

The perks don't stop there, you can get exclusive access to discounts, newsletters, and great free content in your inbox daily

Follow these simple steps to get the benefits:

1. Scan the QR code or visit the link below

https://packt.link/free-ebook/978-1-83546-854-8

2. Submit your proof of purchase
3. That's it! We'll send your free PDF and other benefits to your email directly